Remember Me...

One Demanded Works. One Offered Faith.

Chaplain Kevin C. Malley, D.D.

Remember Me... One Demanded Works. One Offered Faith.

Copyright © 2026 by Kevin C. Malley

All rights reserved.

Scripture quotations are from the World English Bible (WEB), a public domain modern English translation of the Holy Bible.

Printed in the United States of America

First Edition: 2026

ISBN: 979-8-218-84472-1

Published by Malley & Associates

www.chaplainmalley.com

In Loving Memory of Kathleen and Shirley

They Believed......

DEDICATION

To my daughters Kate and Kara,

to my grandchildren Connor, Kendall, and Finnagan,

and to my sons-in-law, past, present, and future,

Jason, Noel, and David.

To the men I grew up with in Blue Island, Illinois—

fertile soil for raising humans.

Your lives have proved it.

John 8:32

"You will know the truth, and the truth will make you free."

To everyone who has ever stood at a graveside

wondering if a loved one made it.

And to everyone still living

who needs to know the truth

while the door is still open.

About the Author

Kevin Malley knows what it's like to stand at a graveside and wonder. *Did they make it?* That question is part of what drives his teaching ministry today.

Raised in Blue Island, Illinois, Malley served as a Captain in the United States Army before spending years in corporate America. He holds a Doctorate in Divinity from North Central Theological Seminary and is an ordained minister and chaplain.

But credentials don't drive this book. A conviction does — that everyone deserves to know what Scripture says about salvation, death, and eternity while the door is still open.

He lives with his family in Freeport, Illinois.

www.chaplainmalley.com

CONTENTS

Chapter 10: The Urgency of Now

CONCLUSION

Chapter 11: Which Man Are You?

APPENDICES

A WORD TO THE READER

This book is filled with Scripture, and intentionally so.

These pages are not meant to offer opinions about death, eternity, and salvation. They are meant to show what God has already said.

But a request: Don't simply take our word for it.

Acts 17:10-11

"The brothers immediately sent Paul and Silas away by night to Berea. When they arrived, they went into the Jewish synagogue. Now these were more noble than those in Thessalonica, in that they received the word with all readiness of mind, examining the Scriptures daily to see whether these things were so."

The Bereans heard the teaching, even from the apostle Paul himself, and then they opened the Scriptures to verify it. They were called "more noble" for doing so.

Every passage quoted in this book is there to be looked up, read in context, and tested. Get a Bible. Check the references. See whether these things are so.

> "Beloved, don't believe every spirit, but test the spirits, whether they are of God, because many false prophets have gone out into the world."

The goal of this book is not to create dependence on any human teacher. The goal is to point to the Word of God so that anyone can know, for themselves, who they are, where they're going, and why they're still here.

A Note on Scripture

All Scripture quotations in this book are from the World English Bible (WEB), a modern English translation in the public domain. The WEB is based on the 1901 American Standard Version, updated for contemporary readers while maintaining faithfulness to the original Hebrew and Greek texts.

Scripture references are marked in red for easy reference. Looking up every passage and comparing translations is encouraged. The truth of God's Word will stand up to scrutiny.

Read with a Bible open. Test everything. And let the Scriptures speak.

A Note on Paul

Throughout this book, we quote heavily from the apostle Paul. Some may wonder why.

Paul was not one of the original twelve disciples. He never walked with Jesus during His earthly ministry. In fact, he was an enemy, a persecutor, "breathing threats and slaughter" against believers (Acts 9:1).

But Paul was trained directly by the resurrected Christ, receiving the gospel by divine revelation, not human teaching:

Galatians 1:11-12

> "For I make known to you, brothers, concerning the Good News which was preached by me, that it is not according to man. For I didn't receive it from man, nor was I taught it, but it came to me through revelation of Jesus Christ."

He was commissioned specifically as the apostle to the Gentiles:

Romans 11:13

> "For I speak to you who are Gentiles. Since then as I am an apostle to Gentiles, I glorify my ministry."

And the original apostles confirmed his gospel at the Jerusalem Council (Acts 15), where Peter declared that Jews and Gentiles alike are saved by grace through faith, and James gave the verdict to not burden the Gentiles with the Law.

When we quote Paul, we quote one who spoke with the authority of Christ Himself, validated by those who walked with Christ before the resurrection. (See Appendix H for a visual timeline of Paul's ministry.)

INTRODUCTION
The Hill

Before we begin, consider one scene.

If this scene makes sense, really makes sense, everything else in this book will follow.

A hill outside Jerusalem. Three crosses against the sky. Three men dying.

In the middle hangs Jesus of Nazareth. The Word made flesh. The Lamb of God. At that very moment, He is bearing the sins of the world. At that very moment, He is defeating death itself.

On one side hangs a criminal. Guilty. Condemned. Crucified for his crimes.

On the other side hangs another criminal. Equally guilty. Equally condemned. Equally close to Christ.

Same hill. Same hour. Same opportunity.

Watch what happens.

Luke 23:39-43

"One of the criminals who was hanged insulted him, saying, "If you are the Christ, save yourself and us!" But the other answered, and

11

rebuking him said, "Don't you even fear God, seeing you are under the same condemnation? And we indeed justly, for we receive the due reward for our deeds, but this man has done nothing wrong." He said to Jesus, "Lord, remember me when you come into your Kingdom." Jesus said to him, "Assuredly I tell you, today you will be with me in Paradise.""

Two criminals. Two responses. Two destinies.

One scoffed and heard silence.

One trusted and heard Paradise.

That's the gospel. Right there. In one scene.

The man who believed had no good works. No religious credentials. No time to prove himself. His hands were nailed to a cross, so he couldn't even fold them in prayer.

He had nothing but faith in the One dying beside him.

And it was enough.

"Today you will be with me in Paradise."

Not someday. Not if he earned it. Not after a review of his record.

Today.

This scene will be the anchor throughout this book. We will return to it again and again. Because everything needed to understand salvation, to understand who we are, where we're going, and why we're still here, is right there on that hill.

Christ in the middle. The dividing line of all humanity.

A man who trusted on one side.

A man who scoffed on the other.

The question this book will answer, the question every life will answer, is simple:

Which man?

A Note on Scripture and Narrative

This book weaves together two threads: Scripture and narrative.

Scripture, the quoted Word of God, is set apart and marked. These are the words that carry divine authority. These are the words through which faith comes (Romans 10:17).

The narrative sections are my attempt to paint the scenes that Scripture describes. When I imagine what the man on the cross saw, heard, or felt, I am not claiming inspiration. I am offering imagination in service of understanding.

Think of it this way: Scripture is the map. The narrative is the journey. The map tells you exactly where to go. The journey helps you feel the ground beneath your feet.

Trust the map. Let the journey bring it to life.

The Hill

Luke 23:32-33

"Two others also, who were criminals, were led
with him to be put to death. When they came
to the place that is called The Skull, they
crucified him there with the criminals, one on
the right and the other on the left."

---

33 AD. Jerusalem. A hill called Golgotha.

The Roman soldiers work quickly. They have
done this before. Thousands of times. The
crossbeam. The nails. The ropes. The lifting of the
beam into place.

Three men are being executed today.

The one in the middle draws the largest crowd.
His sign reads Jesus of Nazareth, the King of the

Jews. The religious leaders demanded a different wording. Pilate refused.

On either side, two criminals. The charges are not recorded. The names are not given. History does not remember who they were.

But history will never forget what they did.

Luke 23:34

"Jesus said, Father, forgive them, for they do not know what they are doing."

The man on the left hears this. Forgive them? The soldiers just drove nails through His wrists. The crowd is mocking Him. The religious leaders are spitting insults.

And He is asking His Father to forgive them?

The criminal has stolen. He has lied. He has probably killed. But he has never, not once, forgiven anyone who wronged him. He does not understand this man in the middle.

He does not want to understand.

Matthew 27:44

"The robbers also who were crucified with him cast on him the same reproach."

Both criminals join the mockery. At first.

The crowd is jeering. The leaders are taunting. Even the soldiers are playing along. It is easy to pile on. Easy to direct the rage outward. Easy to forget, for a moment, that death is coming.

If you are the King of the Jews, save yourself!

He saved others; let him save himself!

If you are the Christ, save yourself and us!

The man on the left keeps shouting. Every breath costs him. Every word is agony. But he keeps shouting.

The man on the right goes quiet.

Luke 23:39

"One of the criminals who was hanged insulted him, saying, If you are the Christ, save yourself and us!"

The man on the left is still demanding. Still mocking. Still insisting that if Jesus is who He claims to be, He should prove it. Come down from the cross. End this suffering. Save us all.

But something is shifting on the right side of the hill.

Luke 23:40-41

"But the other answered, and rebuking him said, Do you not even fear God, seeing you are under the same condemnation? And we indeed justly, for we receive the due reward for our deeds, but this man has done nothing wrong."

The man on the right speaks. It costs him dearly, every word stolen from lungs that are slowly filling with fluid.

But he has to say it.

Do you not even fear God?

We are dying. All three of us. In hours, maybe minutes, we will stand before the Almighty. And you are still mocking?

We deserve this. We earned these crosses. But this man...

He turns his head. He looks at Jesus. The blood. The thorns. The wounds.

This man has done nothing wrong.

How does he know?

Was he in the crowd when Jesus taught on the hillside? Did he see the loaves and fish multiplied? Did he hear the rumors of Lazarus walking out of the tomb?

Scripture does not say. But somehow, in this final hour, the criminal on the right sees what the religious leaders refuse to see.

This is not a failed messiah. This is not a blasphemer. This is the Son of God.

And He is dying on purpose.

Luke 23:42

"He said, Jesus, remember me when you come into your Kingdom."

The man on the right does not ask to be saved from the cross. He does not demand a miracle. He does not negotiate terms.

He simply asks to be remembered.

Remember me.

It is a plea. A prayer. A desperate reach across the space between two crosses.

When you come into your Kingdom.

He sees it now. This is not the end. This is the door. Jesus has a Kingdom, not of this world, but real. Eternal. Coming.

Luke 23:43

"Jesus said to him, Assuredly, I tell you, today you will be with me in Paradise."

Today.

Not someday. Not after purgatory. Not after penance. Not after years of proving himself.

Today.

Before the sun sets. Before the bodies are taken down. Before the Sabbath begins.

The criminal who deserved hell will walk into Paradise. The man with nothing to offer but faith will stand with Christ before the day is over.

Luke 23:44-46

> "It was now about the sixth hour, and darkness came over the whole land until the ninth hour. The sun was darkened, and the veil of the temple was torn in two. Jesus, crying with a loud voice, said, Father, into your hands I commit my spirit! Having said this, he breathed his last."

The sky goes dark. At noon. For three hours.

The man on the left hangs in the blackness, still breathing, still refusing.

Then Jesus cries out. The earth shakes. The rocks split. The veil of the temple, sixty feet tall, four inches thick, tears from top to bottom.

Not from bottom to top, as if by human hands.

From top to bottom. God Himself is tearing it open.

Matthew 27:52-54

"The tombs were opened, and many bodies of the saints who had fallen asleep were raised; and coming out of the tombs after his resurrection, they entered into the holy city and appeared to many. Now the centurion and those who were with him watching Jesus, when they saw the earthquake and the things that were done, feared exceedingly, saying, Truly this was the Son of God."

The dead are walking out of their graves.

The Roman centurion, a pagan soldier who has crucified hundreds, falls to his knees.

Truly this was the Son of God.

A Roman sees it. The religious leaders refuse to see it.

And the man on the left?

He saw the darkness. He felt the earthquake. He watched the centurion fall.

And still he did not believe.

Hours later, both criminals are dead.

One opened his eyes in Paradise. Just as promised. Today.

One opened his eyes in darkness. A different kind of darkness. The kind that does not end.

Same hill. Same hour. Same Savior within arms reach.

One demanded works and heard silence.

One offered faith and heard Paradise.

The only difference was a decision.

This is not a parable. This is history.

These men lived. These crosses stood. These words were spoken.

And the same offer made to a dying criminal two thousand years ago is still open today.

The question is the same: What will you do with Jesus?

The door is open. But it will not be forever.

PART ONE

THE PROBLEM

CHAPTER ONE

The Myth

Funerals reveal what people believe.

Standing at gravesides, hugging grieving families, sitting in quiet rooms where sorrow hangs heavy, certain phrases surface again and again:

"She's in a better place now."

"He's looking down on us from heaven."

"She was such a good person, I'm sure she's with God."

"He's at peace now."

Hope mixed with uncertainty. Comfort mixed with confusion. Love mixed with fear.

Behind those words hide the questions people are afraid to ask out loud:

"Did she make it?"

"Was he good enough?"

"How can anyone really know?"

These questions haunt people because they don't know what the Bible actually teaches. They've absorbed a picture of the afterlife from movies, cartoons, jokes, and cultural assumptions, a picture that feels true because everyone seems to believe it.

But it isn't true. Not one part of it.

And because the myth is believed, lives are built on it. People don't know who they are. They don't know where they're going. They don't know why they're here.

What is this myth? And what is the truth?

The Popular Picture

Ask the average person, even the average churchgoer, what happens when someone dies. The answer usually sounds something like this:

A person dies.

The soul floats up toward heaven.

At the pearly gates, St. Peter stands with a big book, or maybe a clipboard.

He looks up the name and reviews the life.

If the good deeds outweigh the bad, the person is in.

If not, it's hell.

This picture is so deeply embedded in Western culture that most people assume it comes straight from the Bible.

It doesn't.

The "pearly gates" image comes from Revelation 21, but that passage describes the New Jerusalem at the end of all things, after the final resurrection and the last judgment. It's not a checkpoint at the moment of death.

The "St. Peter at the gate" idea comes from a misreading of Matthew 16, where Jesus gives Peter "the keys of the kingdom." But Jesus was talking about Peter's authority in the church on earth, not a job as heaven's doorman. Nowhere in Scripture does Peter stand at any gate judging the dead.

And the "good person" standard, deeds weighed on a scale, good versus bad, that's not Christianity at all.

It's moralism. It's karma. It's the default religion of the human heart.

But it's not what God says.

Why the Myth Is Deadly

When the myth is believed, one of two things happens.

Some become arrogant. "I'm basically a good person. I'm better than most. I don't murder, I don't steal, I try to be nice. I'll be fine."

Others live in anxiety. "Am I good enough? Have I done enough? How can I ever know for sure? What if I don't make the cut?"

Arrogance or anxiety. Pride or fear. Both responses come from the same lie, that entrance into God's presence depends on moral performance.

But there's an even deeper problem.

If salvation is about being good enough to get into heaven when death comes, then life becomes a waiting game. Waiting to die. Hoping to be good enough. Missing the entire point.

Because Christianity is not primarily about what happens at death.

It's about what happens at belief.

The Real Question

The question isn't: "Where will I go when I die?"

The question is: "Where am I right now?"

According to Scripture, every person on earth belongs to one of two kingdoms. Not "will belong," but belongs. Right now.

Colossians 1:13-14

> "He has delivered us from the power of darkness and translated us into the Kingdom of the Son of his love, in whom we have our redemption, the forgiveness of our sins."

Notice the tense. Past tense. "Has delivered." "Translated." Already done.

Those who have trusted Christ have been delivered from the power of darkness. They have been translated, transferred, relocated, moved, into the Kingdom of God's Son.

This isn't a ticket for a future destination. It's a change of address. A change of citizenship. A change of kingdoms.

Right now.

John 5:24

> "Most certainly I tell you, he who hears my word and believes him who sent me has eternal life, and doesn't come into judgment, but has passed out of death into life."

"Has eternal life." Not "will have." Has.

"Has passed out of death into life." Not "will pass." Has passed.

The transfer doesn't happen at death. It happens at belief.

One Hill, Three Crosses

To see all of this clearly, to see the myth demolished and the truth revealed, return to the scene we opened with.

A hill outside Jerusalem. Three crosses. Three men dying.

In the middle hangs Jesus of Nazareth. The Word made flesh. The Lamb of God. The Son of the living God. At that very moment, bearing the sins of the world. At that very moment, defeating death itself.

On one side hangs a criminal. Guilty. Condemned. Crucified for his crimes.

On the other side hangs another criminal. Equally guilty. Equally condemned. Equally close to Christ.

Same hill. Same hour. Same opportunity.

Two responses. Two destinies.

The Man Who Scoffed

Consider the first man.

He knew who Jesus claimed to be. "If you are the Christ," he said. He'd heard the claim. This wasn't ignorance. He knew enough to mock.

He wanted rescue on his own terms. "Save yourself and us!" Get us down from these crosses. Fix the immediate problem. He wanted physical deliverance, not spiritual transformation.

He used his dying breaths to insult the only One who could save him.

And consider his proximity. He was feet away from Christ. Literally feet. He heard every word Jesus spoke. He saw how Jesus suffered. He was closer to the Savior than most people will ever be.

And it wasn't enough.

Because proximity is not faith. Knowledge is not trust. Being near Christ is not the same as receiving Christ.

The first man died as he lived, scoffing, demanding, rejecting. And when he breathed his last, there was no promise for him. Only silence.

The Man Who Trusted

Now consider the second man.

Same guilt. "We receive the due reward for our deeds," he admitted. He wasn't claiming to be a good person. He wasn't arguing that he deserved anything.

Same condemnation. Same cross. Same nails. Same agony.

But a different response.

He rebuked the other criminal. "Don't you even fear God?" He recognized the gravity of the moment. He recognized who was hanging beside him.

He acknowledged his own guilt. "We indeed justly." No excuses. No blaming circumstances. No claiming his good outweighed his bad.

He recognized Jesus for who He was. "This man has done nothing wrong." In a world screaming for Christ's death, this dying man declared His innocence.

And then came the request that changed everything:

"Lord, remember me when you come into your Kingdom."

Not "get me down from this cross." Not "fix my circumstances." Not "give me what I deserve."

Just: "Remember me."

He had nothing to offer. No good works. No religious credentials. No money, no influence, no time to prove himself. His hands were nailed to a cross.

He had nothing but faith in the One dying beside him.

And Jesus answered:

"Assuredly I tell you, today you will be with me in Paradise."

Today. Not "after you've proven yourself." Not "if you do enough good to balance the scales." Not "we'll see how things work out."

Today. Paradise. Guaranteed.

* * *

Imagine the Scene

Now, for the sake of the popular misconception, imagine what happens next.

> He takes his last breath on that cross. His body is broken. His crimes are real. His hands have stolen. His life has been wasted. He has nothing to show for his years on earth except a death sentence and a moment of faith.
>
> But he heard the words of Christ: "Today you will be with me in Paradise."

35

And now, if the popular myth were true, he arrives at the pearly gates.

There stands a gatekeeper. Perhaps St. Peter himself. Clipboard in hand. The Book of Life open on a golden podium.

The gatekeeper looks at this man. Ragged. Broken. The wounds from the nails still visible in his hands. No halo. No flowing robes. No credentials.

"Who are you?"

He swallows.

"I... I was a criminal. I was crucified today."

The gatekeeper frowns. Flips through the pages. Runs a finger down long columns of names and deeds. Looks up with narrowed eyes.

"I see. And what makes you think you belong here?"

He has no answer.

"What good works have you done? What righteousness do you bring? What have you earned?"

He opens his mouth, but nothing comes out. He has no defense. No resume. No list of achievements. He was a sinner every day of his life, and he knows it.

The gatekeeper leans forward.

"So, by what right do you enter Paradise?"

And he, with nothing else to say, simply turns.

He points to the One on the Throne.

The One with the scars in His hands.

The One who hung on the middle cross.

He points at Christ and says...

"He said I could come."

* * *

And that settles it.

Not because he was good enough. He wasn't.

Not because his good deeds outweighed his bad. They didn't.

Not because he earned anything. He earned death.

But because the King of that Kingdom had spoken. And what the King declares, no gatekeeper can question. No angel can overturn. No record of sins can contradict.

"Today you will be with me in Paradise."

He brought nothing but the word of Christ.

And the word of Christ was everything.

The Dividing Line

Three crosses. Christ in the middle.

The middle cross is the dividing line of all humanity.

On one side, the man who trusted. He heard Paradise.

On the other side, the man who scoffed. He heard silence.

Same proximity. Same opportunity. Same dying hour.

Different responses. Different eternities.

The difference wasn't their background, both were criminals. The difference wasn't their guilt, both were condemned. The difference wasn't their location, both were within arm's reach of Jesus.

The difference was faith.

One trusted. One didn't.

One received. One rejected.

One entered the Kingdom. One didn't.

And the One in the middle, the Word made flesh, the Lamb of God, the King of kings, He is the dividing line between eternal life and eternal death.

What Most People Miss

The man who believed's story is usually told as a story about death. About getting into heaven at the last second. About the door being open even for a criminal.

And that's true, as far as it goes.

But the real miracle isn't just what happened when he died. It's what happened while he was still alive on that cross.

The moment he trusted Christ, in that moment, he was transferred.

He didn't have to wait until he died to enter the Kingdom. He entered it while he was still breathing.

He was still hanging on a cross. Still in agony. Still a criminal in the eyes of Rome. But in the eyes of God, everything had changed.

He had passed from death to life.

He had been delivered from the domain of darkness.

He had become a citizen of the Kingdom of God's beloved Son.

Right there. On that cross. Before his heart stopped.

He only had minutes to live as a citizen of that Kingdom. But he was a citizen nonetheless.

And anyone who trusts Christ becomes one too.

Not at death. Now.

Not someday. Today.

The question isn't where someone will go at death. The question is where they are right now.

The Myth and the Truth

The myth says: Be good enough, and St. Peter will let you into heaven when you die.

The truth says: Trust Christ and be transferred into His Kingdom right now.

The myth says: Performance determines destiny.

The truth says: Christ's word determines destiny, and He has already spoken.

The myth says: Hope to make the cut.

The truth says: "Assuredly I tell you, today you will be with me in Paradise."

The myth leaves people uncertain, anxious, waiting to find out.

The truth offers a King who speaks with authority, and what He declares, nothing in heaven or earth can undo.

* * *

In the chapters ahead, we will trace what Scripture actually teaches, about death and life, about the cross and the Kingdom, about who we are and where we're going.

But we'll keep coming back to that hill. Those three crosses. The One in the middle.

Because everything flows from there.

The man who scoffed shows what proximity without faith produces: nothing.

The man who trusted shows what faith without works receives: everything.

And Christ in the middle shows the One who has all authority in heaven and on earth, the One whose word is the final word.

"He said I could come."

That's the gospel.

Let's keep going.

CHAPTER TWO

What Scripture Reveals

Before going further, we need to see what Scripture actually teaches about death and the afterlife.

Most people, even lifelong churchgoers, have never studied this carefully. They've picked up fragments from sermons, songs, and sympathy cards. They've filled in the gaps with assumptions.

But the Bible speaks clearly on this subject. And what it says is different from what most people expect.

Let's trace the storyline from the Old Testament through the New.

The Old Testament: Sheol

In the Old Testament, the Hebrew word for the place of the dead is Sheol. It appears over sixty times in the Hebrew Scriptures.

Sheol is not heaven. It's not hell, at least not in the way most people think of hell. It's the shadowy realm of the dead, where all people went when they died, righteous and wicked alike.

Psalm 89:48

> "What man is he who shall live and not see death, who shall deliver his soul from the power of Sheol?"

No one escapes. Death comes for everyone, and Sheol receives them all.

Ecclesiastes 9:10

> "Whatever your hand finds to do, do it with your might; for there is no work, nor plan, nor knowledge, nor wisdom, in Sheol, where you are going."

Sheol is described as a place of silence, darkness, inactivity. The dead there are called "shades," dim, weakened versions of their former selves.

Isaiah 14:9-10

> "Sheol from beneath has moved for you to meet you at your coming. It stirs up the departed spirits for you, even all the rulers of the earth. It has raised up from their thrones all the kings of the nations. They all will answer

and ask you, 'Have you also become as weak
as we are? Have you become like us?'"

The dead in Sheol have some awareness, some identity, but they are weak, shadowy, cut off.

And here is the troubling part for those in the Old Testament: Sheol seemed to be a place of separation from God.

Psalm 6:5

"For in death there is no memory of you. In Sheol, who shall give you thanks?"

Psalm 88:10-12

"Do you show wonders to the dead? Do the departed spirits rise up and praise you? Is your loving kindness declared in the grave? Or your faithfulness in Destruction? Are your wonders made known in the dark? Or your righteousness in the land of forgetfulness?"

This is why death was so feared in the Old Testament. It wasn't just the end of life on earth. It was descent into shadows, silence, separation.

The Emerging Hope

But Sheol was not the final word.

Even in the Old Testament, there are glimpses of something more. Hints that death would not have the last say. Whispers of resurrection.

Psalm 16:10

> "For you will not leave my soul in Sheol,
> neither will you allow your holy one to see
> corruption."

David wrote these words. But they pointed beyond David, to the One who would conquer death itself. Peter quoted this very passage at Pentecost, declaring that it was fulfilled in Christ's resurrection.

Psalm 49:15

> "But God will redeem my soul from the power
> of Sheol, for he will receive me."

Redemption from Sheol. Being received by God. The hope is there, faint but real.

Isaiah 25:8

> "He has swallowed up death forever! The Lord
> Yahweh will wipe away tears from off all faces.

He will take away the reproach of his people
from off all the earth, for Yahweh has spoken
it."

Death swallowed up forever. Tears wiped away. This is not
Sheol. This is victory.

Isaiah 26:19

"Your dead shall live. My dead bodies shall
arise. Awake and sing, you who dwell in the
dust; for your dew is like the dew of herbs, and
the earth will cast out the departed spirits."

Bodies rising. The dead living again. The dust awakening to
sing.

And then, one of the clearest statements in the Old
Testament:

Daniel 12:2

"Many of those who sleep in the dust of the
earth will awake, some to everlasting life, and
some to shame and everlasting contempt."

Two destinies. Everlasting life and everlasting contempt.
Not everyone going to the same shadowy Sheol forever, but
resurrection, and then separation.

The Old Testament ends with hope on the horizon. But the full picture was yet to come.

The New Testament: Clarity

When we turn to the New Testament, the picture becomes much clearer. Jesus and the apostles reveal what the Old Testament only hinted at.

And they give us new vocabulary.

Hades

In the Greek New Testament, Hades is roughly equivalent to the Old Testament's Sheol, the realm of the dead.

But with a crucial difference: Hades now has divisions.

Remember the rich man and Lazarus? Jesus pulled back the curtain and showed what Hades looks like:

Luke 16:22-26

> "The beggar died, and he was carried away by the angels to Abraham's bosom. The rich man also died and was buried. In Hades, he lifted up his eyes, being in torment, and saw Abraham far off, and Lazarus at his bosom. He cried and said, 'Father Abraham, have mercy on me, and send Lazarus, that he may dip the

tip of his finger in water and cool my tongue! For I am in anguish in this flame.' But Abraham said, 'Son, remember that you, in your lifetime, received your good things, and Lazarus, in the same way, bad things. But now here he is comforted and you are in anguish. Besides all this, between us and you there is a great gulf fixed, that those who want to pass from here to you are not able, and that no one may cross over from there to us.'"

Two places. One of comfort, Abraham's bosom. One of torment, flame and anguish. And between them, a great chasm that cannot be crossed.

Hades is not the final state. It's the waiting place, where the dead await resurrection and final judgment.

But even in Hades, the separation has already begun.

Gehenna

When Jesus spoke of final judgment, the ultimate destiny of the wicked, He used a different word: Gehenna.

Gehenna was the name of a valley outside Jerusalem, the Valley of Hinnom, where trash was burned and, in ancient times, child sacrifice had been practiced. It became a symbol of judgment and destruction.

Jesus used this word twelve times. He didn't soften it.

Matthew 10:28

> "Don't be afraid of those who kill the body, but
> are not able to kill the soul. Rather, fear him
> who is able to destroy both soul and body in
> Gehenna."

Mark 9:47-48

> "If your eye causes you to stumble, cast it out.
> It is better for you to enter into God's Kingdom
> with one eye, rather than having two eyes to be
> cast into Gehenna, where their worm doesn't
> die, and the fire is not quenched."

Unquenchable fire. The worm that doesn't die. Jesus spoke
of Gehenna with stark, terrifying imagery.

This is not a temporary holding place. This is final
judgment. This is the destination that awaits those who die
without Christ.

Paradise

But there is another destination, for those who trust in
Christ.

Remember what Jesus said to the man on the cross?

Luke 23:43

"Jesus said to him, 'Assuredly I tell you, today you will be with me in Paradise.'"

Paradise. The same word used for the Garden of Eden in the Greek translation of the Old Testament. A place of life, beauty, communion with God.

Paul spoke of Paradise as well:

2 Corinthians 12:4

"...how he was caught up into Paradise, and heard unspeakable words, which it is not lawful for a man to utter."

Paradise is where believers go when they die. Not the shadowy Sheol of the Old Testament. Not the tormenting side of Hades. But Paradise, the presence of Christ.

Philippians 1:23

"But I am hard pressed between the two, having the desire to depart and be with Christ, which is far better."

Paul had no fear of death. To depart and be with Christ, that was "far better."

2 Corinthians 5:8

> "We are courageous, I say, and are willing rather to be absent from the body, and to be at home with the Lord."

Absent from the body, at home with the Lord. This is what awaits the believer at death.

But This Is Not the End

Paradise is wonderful. Being with Christ is far better than this life. But it is still not the final state.

The New Testament hope is not just "going to heaven when you die." It's bigger than that.

The ultimate hope is resurrection.

1 Corinthians 15:51-53

> "Behold, I tell you a mystery. We will not all sleep, but we will all be changed, in a moment, in the twinkling of an eye, at the last trumpet. For the trumpet will sound and the dead will be raised incorruptible, and we will be

changed. For this perishable body must
become imperishable, and this mortal must put
on immortality."

The dead will be raised. Not just souls in Paradise, but
bodies raised from the grave. Transformed. Imperishable.
Immortal.

1 Thessalonians 4:16-17

"For the Lord himself will descend from
heaven with a shout, with the voice of the
archangel and with God's trumpet. The dead in
Christ will rise first, then we who are alive,
who are left, will be caught up together with
them in the clouds to meet the Lord in the air.
So we will be with the Lord forever."

This is the Christian hope. Not disembodied souls floating
on clouds forever. Not just "going to heaven." But
resurrection, bodies raised, transformed, reunited with
glorified souls, and then life forever in God's renewed
creation.

Revelation 21:1-4

"I saw a new heaven and a new earth, for the
first heaven and the first earth have passed
away, and the sea is no more. I saw the holy

city, New Jerusalem, coming down out of heaven from God, prepared like a bride adorned for her husband. I heard a loud voice out of heaven saying, 'Behold, God's dwelling is with people; and he will dwell with them, and they will be his people, and God himself will be with them as their God. He will wipe away every tear from their eyes. Death will be no more; neither will there be mourning, nor crying, nor pain any more. The first things have passed away.'"

God dwelling with His people. No more death. No more tears. No more mourning, crying, or pain. This is where history is headed. This is the final destination for those who belong to Christ.

Back to the Hill

Now, with all of this in mind, return to the three crosses.

Christ in the middle. Two men on either side.

The man who trusted heard: "Today you will be with me in Paradise." That very day, his soul was with Christ. And when Christ returns, his body will be raised. He will live forever in the new creation.

The man who scoffed heard: silence. When he died, he went to Hades, to torment, to waiting. And when the final judgment comes, he will be raised only to face the lake of fire.

Same hill. Same hour. Same opportunity.

Different responses. Different eternities.

The Old Testament saints looked forward to this moment, the moment when death would be defeated, when Sheol would release its captives, when resurrection would come.

The man on the cross was the first to receive the promise from the lips of Christ Himself.

"Today you will be with me in Paradise."

And that promise stands for everyone who trusts in Him.

* * *

Now we know what Scripture reveals about death and the afterlife. The shadowy Sheol of the Old Testament. The divided Hades of the New. Paradise for believers. Gehenna for unbelievers. Resurrection for all, some to everlasting life, some to everlasting contempt.

But we haven't yet talked about what made the difference.

Why did the man who believed go to Paradise?

Was it because he was good? No, he admitted his guilt.

Was it because he earned it? No, he had nothing to offer.

Was it because of something he did? No, his hands were nailed to a cross.

It was because of the One on the middle cross. And what that One accomplished there.

That's where we turn next.

PART TWO

THE CROSS

CHAPTER THREE

The Domain of Darkness

There is something most people don't understand about the human condition.

The common assumption is that people are basically good. A little flawed, maybe. Prone to mistakes. But fundamentally decent, and if they just try hard enough, they'll be fine.

The Bible tells a different story.

According to Scripture, human beings are not just flawed. They are captive. Enslaved. Prisoners in a kingdom they didn't choose, under a ruler they cannot see.

Before we can understand what Christ accomplished at the cross, we have to understand what He was saving us from.

It's worse than most people think.

The God of This World

Paul wrote to the Corinthians about why some people reject the gospel. His explanation is startling:

> "Even if our Good News is veiled, it is veiled in
> those who are dying, in whom the god of this
> world has blinded the minds of the
> unbelieving, that the light of the Good News of
> the glory of Christ, who is the image of God,
> should not dawn on them."

There is a "god of this world." Not the true God, a false god.
A usurper. An enemy.

And this god has blinded the minds of unbelievers.

The reason people don't believe isn't just that they
haven't heard the gospel clearly. It isn't just that they're
stubborn or foolish. There is an active force, a malevolent
intelligence, working to keep them from seeing the truth.

They are blinded. And the one who blinds them is
called "the god of this world."

The Prince of the Power of the Air

Paul describes him further in Ephesians:

Ephesians 2:1-3

> "You were made alive when you were dead in
> transgressions and sins, in which you once
> walked according to the course of this world,

according to the prince of the power of the air, the spirit who now works in the children of disobedience. We also all once lived among them in the lust of our flesh, doing the desires of the flesh and of the mind, and were by nature children of wrath, even as the rest."

Before coming to Christ, people are:

Dead in transgressions and sins.

Walking according to the course of this world.

Following the prince of the power of the air.

By nature children of wrath.

Not neutral. Not free. Following a prince, a ruler, a spirit who works in the children of disobedience.

This is Satan. The devil. The adversary.

And every unbeliever is under his influence, whether they know it or not.

The Ruler of This World

Jesus Himself spoke of Satan's position:

John 12:31

"Now is the judgment of this world. Now the prince of this world will be cast out."

John 14:30

"I will no more speak much with you, for the prince of the world comes, and he has nothing in me."

John 16:11

"...about judgment, because the prince of this world has been judged."

Three times Jesus called Satan "the prince of this world." Not the prince of hell, the prince of this world. This present age. This current system.

Satan has real authority here. Not ultimate authority, God is still sovereign. But delegated authority, usurped authority, authority that human beings handed over through sin.

When Satan tempted Jesus in the wilderness, he showed Him all the kingdoms of the world and said:

Luke 4:6

> "The devil said to him, 'I will give you all this authority and their glory, for it has been delivered to me, and I give it to whomever I want.'"

Jesus didn't dispute the claim. Satan does have authority over the kingdoms of this world. It was "delivered" to him when Adam and Eve believed his lie and handed over the dominion God had given them.

This is why the world is the way it is. This is why there is so much darkness, so much evil, so much suffering. The prince of this world is a liar and a murderer.

John 8:44

> "You are of your father, the devil, and you want to do the desires of your father. He was a murderer from the beginning, and doesn't stand in the truth, because there is no truth in him. When he speaks a lie, he speaks on his own; for he is a liar, and the father of lies."

Given Over

And here is the terrible progression. Those who continue to reject God are not simply left alone. They are given over.

Romans 1:21-22, 24, 26, 28

> "Because knowing God, they didn't glorify him as God, and didn't give thanks, but became vain in their reasoning, and their senseless heart was darkened. Professing themselves to be wise, they became fools... Therefore God also gave them up in the lusts of their hearts to uncleanness... For this reason, God gave them up to vile passions... Even as they refused to have God in their knowledge, God gave them up to a reprobate mind, to do those things which are not fitting."

Three times: God gave them up. God gave them over.

This is not God actively pushing people into sin. It is God removing His restraining hand. Letting them have what they insist on having. Allowing the darkness to deepen.

First, given over to uncleanness.

Then, given over to vile passions.

Finally, given over to a reprobate mind, a debased mind, a mind that can no longer think clearly about God, about right and wrong, about reality itself.

This is the terrifying end of continued rejection. Not just blindness, but a mind so darkened it cannot find its way back.

The door is open now. But for those who keep refusing, there may come a point when the door closes, not at death, but before it. A heart so hardened it can no longer respond.

This is why the urgency of the gospel is real. Today is the day of salvation. Tomorrow is not guaranteed, and neither is the ability to believe.

Captives Who Don't Know They're Captive

Here is the tragic reality: most unbelievers don't know they're captive.

They think they're free. They think they're making their own choices. They think they're in control of their lives.

But they're walking in darkness, following a ruler they cannot see, blinded to the truth that could set them free.

2 Timothy 2:25-26

> "...in gentleness correcting those who oppose him, perhaps God may give them repentance leading to a full knowledge of the truth, and they may recover themselves out of the devil's snare, having been taken captive by him to do his will."

65

Taken captive by him to do his will.

That's the condition of every person who hasn't trusted Christ. Not free agents choosing their own path. Captives, doing the will of their captor, trapped in a snare they can't even see.

This is why people reject the gospel. This is why they mock Christ. This is why they scoff at the cross.

They're not just making bad decisions. They're blinded. Enslaved. Captive.

They need rescue.

Two Kingdoms

The Bible presents a stark picture: there are two kingdoms, and every person belongs to one or the other.

Colossians 1:13

> "He has delivered us from the power of
> darkness and translated us into the Kingdom
> of the Son of his love."

The power of darkness. The Kingdom of the Son.

Before Christ: the power of darkness.

After Christ: the Kingdom of the Son.

There is no middle ground. No neutral territory. No "basically good people" who belong to neither kingdom.

A person is either in the domain of darkness, under Satan's authority, blinded, captive, or delivered and transferred into the Kingdom of God's Son.

Acts 26:18

> "...to open their eyes, that they may turn from darkness to light and from the power of Satan to God, that they may receive remission of sins and an inheritance among those who are sanctified by faith in me."

This is what salvation is. Not just forgiveness, though it includes that. Not just heaven at death, though it includes that.

Salvation is rescue. Transfer. Deliverance from one kingdom to another.

From darkness to light.

From Satan's power to God's.

The War Behind the War

This means there is more going on than meets the eye.

When someone rejects the gospel, it's not just a human decision. It's a battle.

When someone mocks Christ, it's not just human words. It's the voice of a captor, speaking through them.

When someone walks away from the truth, it's not just free choice. It's blindness, spiritual blindness inflicted by the god of this world.

Ephesians 6:12

> "For our wrestling is not against flesh and
> blood, but against the principalities, against the
> powers, against the world's rulers of the
> darkness of this age, and against the spiritual
> forces of wickedness in the heavenly places."

Principalities. Powers. Rulers of darkness. Spiritual forces of wickedness.

This is what we're up against. Not just human ignorance. Not just cultural trends. Not just philosophical arguments.

An organized kingdom of darkness, led by a prince who has been deceiving humanity since the Garden of Eden.

And apart from Christ, every human being is on his side, whether they know it or not.

Back to the Hill

Now return to the three crosses.

On the surface: three men dying. Roman soldiers gambling. A crowd watching. An execution.

But behind the scene, in the spiritual realm, a war was being fought.

The prince of this world thought he was winning. The Son of God, defeated. The Messiah, crucified. The hope of the world, dying on a cross.

Satan had blinded the crowds. He had entered Judas. He had worked through the religious leaders and the Roman government. Everything was going according to his plan.

Or so he thought.

He didn't understand that the cross was not his victory. It was his defeat.

He didn't understand that by putting Christ to death, he was sealing his own doom.

He didn't understand that the blood being shed on that middle cross was the very thing that would break his power forever.

And look at the two men.

The one who scoffed, he was still in the domain of darkness. Still blinded. Still captive. Still doing the will of his captor, mocking Christ with his dying breaths.

The one who believed, in that moment, something broke. The blindness lifted. The chains fell off. He saw who Jesus was, and he trusted Him.

And he was transferred. Right there, on a cross, in his final hour, he was delivered from the power of darkness and translated into the Kingdom of the Son.

"Today you will be with me in Paradise."

That's what rescue sounds like.

* * *

Now we see what we're dealing with.

The human condition is not just "flawed but basically good." It's captivity. Blindness. Slavery to a prince who hates God and hates everyone made in God's image.

Every unbeliever is his prisoner.

Every person who hasn't trusted Christ is walking in darkness, following the course of this world, doing the will of a master they cannot see.

They need more than good advice. They need more than moral improvement. They need more than religion.

They need rescue.

They need someone to invade enemy territory, break the chains, open the prison doors, and set the captives free.

And that is exactly what Christ came to do.

1 John 3:8

> "...The Son of God was revealed for this
> purpose: to destroy the works of the devil."

The works of the devil, the blindness, the captivity, the lies, the death, that's what Jesus came to destroy.

And He did it on the cross.

That's the next chapter.

CHAPTER FOUR

Victory at the Cross

It looked like defeat.

The Son of God, arrested. Beaten. Mocked. Stripped naked. Nailed to a cross between two criminals. Dying in agony while His enemies watched and laughed.

His disciples had fled. His movement seemed finished. Everything He had built for three years was crumbling in a single afternoon.

Anyone standing at the foot of that cross would have seen failure. Tragedy. The end.

They would have been wrong.

Because the cross was not Christ's defeat.

It was His victory.

The Hidden Triumph

Paul reveals what was really happening at the cross, what the eyes could not see:

Colossians 2:13-15

"You were dead through your trespasses and the uncircumcision of your flesh. He made you alive together with him, having forgiven us all our trespasses, wiping out the handwriting in ordinances which was against us. He has taken it out of the way, nailing it to the cross. Having disarmed the principalities and powers, he made a show of them openly, triumphing over them in it."

Look at what Christ accomplished:

He made us alive, we who were dead.

He forgave all our trespasses, every sin, wiped clean.

He took the record of our debt and nailed it to the cross, paid in full.

And then, the part most people miss:

He disarmed the principalities and powers.

He made a show of them openly.

He triumphed over them.

The cross was not just about paying for sin. It was about defeating the enemy.

The principalities and powers, the rulers of darkness, the spiritual forces of wickedness, Satan and his demons, they were disarmed at the cross. Stripped of their weapons. Publicly humiliated. Triumphed over.

What looked like Christ's defeat was actually their defeat.

What looked like their victory was actually their undoing.

The One Who Had the Power of Death

The writer of Hebrews explains it further:

Hebrews 2:14-15

> "Since then the children have shared in flesh and blood, he also himself in the same way partook of the same, that through death he might bring to nothing him who had the power of death, that is, the devil, and might deliver all of them who through fear of death were all their lifetime subject to bondage."

The devil had the power of death. He wielded it like a weapon. He used it to keep humanity in bondage, in fear, all their lives.

But Christ entered into flesh and blood, became fully human, so that through His own death, He might bring the devil to nothing.

Bring to nothing. Destroy. Render powerless.

Satan's greatest weapon, death itself, was turned against him. Christ died, yes. But in dying, He destroyed the one who had the power of death.

And now? Those who trust in Christ are delivered from bondage. The fear of death is broken. The weapon has been disarmed.

That's why the man who believed could hear "Today you will be with me in Paradise" and know it was true. Death had lost its power. The one who wielded it had been defeated.

Destroying the Works of the Devil

John states it simply:

1 John 3:8

> "He who sins is of the devil, for the devil has sinned from the beginning. To this end the Son of God was revealed: that he might destroy the works of the devil."

This is why Jesus came. This is why the Son of God was revealed. Not just to teach good morals. Not just to give an example to follow. Not just to show how to live.

He came to destroy the works of the devil.

The blindness, destroyed.

The captivity, broken.

The lies, exposed.

The power of death, shattered.

Every work of the devil, everything Satan had built since the Garden of Eden, was dismantled at the cross.

Even Moses Was Accused

Consider how far the enemy's reach extends.

Moses was one of the greatest figures in Scripture. He spoke with God face to face. He led Israel out of Egypt. He received the Law on Sinai.

And yet, at Moses' death, Satan appeared to claim his body.

Jude 1:9

> "But Michael the archangel, when contending
> with the devil and arguing about the body of
> Moses, didn't dare bring against him an
> abusive condemnation, but said, 'May the Lord
> rebuke you!'"

Why would Satan have any claim on Moses? Because of the murder of the Egyptian (Exodus 2:12). Moses was guilty.

Real sin. Real guilt. And the accuser showed up to make his case.

If Satan could find grounds to accuse Moses, he can find grounds to accuse anyone. No one escapes by being "good enough."

But now consider the contrast. Moses needed Michael the archangel to rebuke Satan on his behalf.

Those who are in Christ have something greater.

Romans 8:33-34

"Who could bring a charge against God's chosen ones? It is God who justifies. Who is he who condemns? It is Christ who died, yes rather, who was raised from the dead, who is at the right hand of God, who also makes intercession for us."

Satan accuses. He still does, he is called "the accuser of the brothers" in Revelation 12:10. But his accusations have no power against those in Christ.

Why? Because Christ died. Christ rose. Christ intercedes.

Moses needed an angel. Believers have the Son of God Himself.

The accuser is silenced. The victory is complete.

How Did Death Defeat Death?

This is the great mystery, and the great wisdom of God.

Satan's plan was to kill Jesus. Remove the threat. End the movement. Destroy the Son of God.

But God's plan was deeper. What looked like Satan's master stroke was actually his fatal mistake.

1 Corinthians 2:7-8

> "But we speak God's wisdom in a mystery, the wisdom that has been hidden, which God foreordained before the worlds for our glory, which none of the rulers of this age has known. For had they known it, they wouldn't have crucified the Lord of glory."

The rulers of this age, the demonic powers behind the human actors, didn't understand what they were doing. If they had known, they would never have crucified Jesus.

Because the cross was a trap.

Satan thought he was destroying Christ. Instead, Christ was destroying him.

Satan thought death would end Jesus. Instead, Jesus ended death.

Satan thought he was winning. Instead, he was handing Christ the very weapon that would defeat him forever.

The blood that flowed from the cross was not the sign of Satan's victory. It was the payment for sin that set the captives free. It was the sacrifice that satisfied divine justice. It was the death that swallowed up death.

1 Corinthians 15:55-57

"Death, where is your sting? Hades, where is your victory? The sting of death is sin, and the power of sin is the law. But thanks be to God, who gives us the victory through our Lord Jesus Christ."

Victory. That's what the cross accomplished. Not defeat, victory.

But Wait, Satan Is Still Active

If Satan was defeated at the cross, why is he still at work? Why does evil still exist? Why are people still being blinded, still being held captive?

This is an important question, and Scripture answers it.

Satan has been defeated, but he has not yet been destroyed. His doom is sealed, but his final destruction is still future.

Think of it like a war.

There is a decisive battle, the turning point, where the outcome becomes certain. And then there is the final surrender, when the war officially ends.

In World War II, D-Day was the decisive battle. June 6, 1944. When the Allies landed at Normandy, the outcome of the war was sealed. Hitler would lose. It was only a matter of time.

But the war didn't end that day. V-E Day, Victory in Europe, came almost a year later, on May 8, 1945. The fighting continued after D-Day. Soldiers still died. Battles were still fought. But the outcome was never in doubt.

The cross was D-Day.

Satan's defeat was sealed. His doom was certain. The outcome of the war was decided.

But we're still living between D-Day and V-Day. The fighting continues. The enemy is still active. But he's fighting a losing battle, and he knows it.

Revelation 12:12

"Therefore rejoice, heavens, and you who dwell in them. Woe to the earth and to the sea, because the devil has gone down to you, having great wrath, knowing that he has but a short time."

Satan has great wrath, because he knows his time is short. He knows he's already lost. He's raging against the inevitable.

But the cross stands. The victory is won. And when Christ returns, the final destruction will come.

Revelation 20:10

"The devil who deceived them was thrown into the lake of fire and sulfur, where the beast and the false prophet are also. They will be tormented day and night forever and ever."

That's V-Day. That's the final end. Satan thrown into the lake of fire forever.

The cross guaranteed it. Christ's return will execute it.

What This Means

Those who have trusted Christ are on the winning side.

Satan may still prowl. He may still accuse. He may still attack. But he cannot have those who belong to Christ. They have been delivered from his domain. They have been transferred to the Kingdom of the Son.

Romans 8:1

"There is therefore now no condemnation to those who are in Christ Jesus."

No condemnation. Not "maybe." Not "if good enough." No condemnation, because Christ already won.

Romans 8:37-39

"No, in all these things we are more than conquerors through him who loved us. For I am persuaded that neither death, nor life, nor angels, nor principalities, nor things present, nor things to come, nor powers, nor height, nor depth, nor any other created thing will be able to separate us from the love of God which is in Christ Jesus our Lord."

More than conquerors. Not barely surviving, more than conquering.

Neither death nor life. Neither angels nor principalities. Neither powers nor any created thing.

Nothing can separate believers from the love of God in Christ Jesus.

Because at the cross, Christ defeated every power that could threaten them.

Back to the Hill

Return one more time to the three crosses.

On that middle cross, something was happening that no one fully understood at the time.

The principalities and powers were being disarmed.

The one who had the power of death was being destroyed.

The works of the devil were being demolished.

The captives were being set free.

The man who believed, in that moment, the chains fell off. The blindness lifted. He was transferred from the domain of darkness into the Kingdom of light. He went from captive to free, from condemned to pardoned, from death to life.

All because of what was happening on the middle cross.

The man who scoffed, he saw the same cross. Heard the same words. Was just as close. But the chains stayed on. The blindness remained. He died in his sins, still captive to the one who had deceived him his whole life.

Same cross. Same opportunity. Different responses.

The cross is the dividing line.

It is where Satan was defeated.

It is where sin was paid for.

It is where death lost its sting.

And it is where everyone must decide: Trust the One who won the victory, or stay in the kingdom that has already lost.

CHAPTER FIVE

Justification by Faith

How is a person made right with God?

This is the most important question anyone can ask. It's the question that determines everything: where someone stands now, where they're going at death, and why they're here in between.

The popular answer, the answer most people assume, is that a person gets right with God by being good. By following the rules. By doing more right than wrong. By being a decent person.

But we've already seen why that answer fails. Human beings are not basically good people who need a little help. They are captives in a kingdom of darkness, dead in their sins, blinded by the god of this world.

They don't need improvement. They need rescue.

And rescue doesn't come by works.

It comes by faith.

The Human Problem

Before we can understand the solution, we have to be honest about the problem.

And the problem is worse than most people think.

Romans 3:10-12

> "As it is written, 'There is no one righteous; no, not one. There is no one who understands. There is no one who seeks after God. They have all turned away. They have together become unprofitable. There is no one who does good, no, not so much as one.'"

No one righteous. Not one.

No one who does good. Not so much as one.

This is God's assessment of humanity. Not "most people are pretty good." Not "a few bad apples ruin it for everyone." No one righteous. No one who does good.

Romans 3:23

> "For all have sinned and fall short of the glory of God."

All have sinned. Not some. Not the really bad ones. All.

And the standard isn't "better than most people." The standard is the glory of God. Perfection. Complete holiness.

Everyone falls short.

This is why the "good person" approach can never work. Even if someone is better than their neighbor, they still fall short of God's glory. Even if they've never committed murder, they still fall short. Even if they go to church every Sunday and give to charity, they still fall short.

The standard isn't "good enough compared to others." The standard is perfect righteousness.

And no one has it.

Works Cannot Save

So what about trying harder? What about the law, following God's commandments? Won't that make someone right with God?

Paul's answer is devastating:

Romans 3:20

> "Because by the works of the law, no flesh will
> be justified in his sight; for through the law
> comes the knowledge of sin."

No flesh will be justified by works of the law.

The law wasn't given to save. The law was given to show sin. It's a mirror that reveals how far short everyone falls. It's a standard that proves no one can measure up.

Galatians 2:16

> "Yet knowing that a man is not justified by the works of the law but through faith in Jesus Christ, we also believed in Christ Jesus, that we might be justified by faith in Christ and not by the works of the law, because no flesh will be justified by the works of the law."

Paul says it three times in one verse: not justified by works of the law.

This is not a minor point. This is the heart of the gospel.

No one can earn their way to God. No one can work their way to righteousness. No one can achieve salvation by moral effort.

If they could, Christ died for nothing.

Galatians 2:21

> "I don't reject the grace of God. For if righteousness is through the law, then Christ died for nothing!"

If being a good person could save, why did Jesus have to die?

The cross proves that works cannot save. If there were any other way, God would not have sent His Son to that hill.

Justified by Faith

So if works can't save, what can?

Paul gives the answer:

Romans 3:21-24

> "But now apart from the law, a righteousness of God has been revealed, being testified by the law and the prophets; even the righteousness of God through faith in Jesus Christ to all and on all those who believe. For there is no distinction, for all have sinned and fall short of the glory of God; being justified freely by his grace through the redemption that is in Christ Jesus."

Righteousness apart from the law. Not by works, by faith.

Justified freely by His grace. Not earned, freely given.

Through the redemption that is in Christ Jesus. Not through human effort, through what Christ did.

This is justification. It's a legal term. It means "declared righteous," not "made righteous slowly over time." Declared righteous, right now, the moment of belief.

Romans 4:4-5

> "Now to him who works, the reward is not counted as grace, but as debt. But to him who doesn't work, but believes in him who justifies the ungodly, his faith is counted for righteousness."

If someone works for it, it's not grace, it's a wage they've earned.

But if someone believes, if they trust in the One who justifies the ungodly, their faith is counted as righteousness.

God justifies the ungodly. Not the godly. Not the good. Not the deserving. The ungodly.

That's who gets saved. People who admit they're ungodly and trust in the One who can make them right.

Abraham: The Pattern

This is not a new idea. This is how it has always been.

Long before the Law was given, long before the temple or the priesthood or the sacrifices, there was Abraham.

Genesis 15:6

"Abram believed Yahweh, and he credited it to him for righteousness."

Abraham believed God. And God credited it to him as righteousness.

Not works. Faith.

Not rituals. Trust.

This was before circumcision. Before the Law. Before any religious system.

Abraham simply believed God's promise. And that faith was counted as righteousness.

Paul makes this the cornerstone of his argument:

Romans 4:3

"For what does the Scripture say? 'Abraham believed God, and it was counted to him for righteousness.'"

And then Paul makes clear this wasn't just for Abraham:

Romans 4:23-25

"Now it was not written that it was counted to him for his sake alone, but for our sake also, to

whom it will be counted, who believe in him
who raised Jesus our Lord from the dead, who
was delivered up for our trespasses, and was
raised for our justification."

Written for us. The same principle. The same faith. The same righteousness credited.

Abraham looked forward to what Christ would do. We look back at what Christ has done. Same faith. Same salvation.

Old Testament to New, the thread of faith runs through it all.

The Great Exchange

But how can this be just? How can God declare sinners righteous? Doesn't that make Him unjust, ignoring sin, pretending it doesn't matter?

No. Because of the cross.

At the cross, an exchange took place, the most important exchange in history:

2 Corinthians 5:21

"For him who knew no sin he made to be sin
on our behalf, so that in him we might become
the righteousness of God."

Christ knew no sin. He was perfectly righteous, the only human who ever lived without sin.

But God made Him to be sin on our behalf. All our sin, every transgression, every failure, every rebellion, was placed on Him. He bore it. He paid for it. He died for it.

And in exchange, we become the righteousness of God in Him.

His righteousness is credited to us. Our sin was credited to Him.

This is the great exchange. This is why God can declare sinners righteous without being unjust. The penalty was paid. The debt was settled. Justice was satisfied, at the cross.

And now, everyone who believes receives the righteousness of Christ as a gift.

By Grace Through Faith

Paul summarizes it clearly:

Ephesians 2:8-9

> "For by grace you have been saved through
> faith, and that not of yourselves; it is the gift of
> God, not of works, that no one would boast."

By grace, unmerited favor. Not deserved.

Through faith, trusting Christ. Not works, faith.

Not of ourselves, not self-generated. It came from outside.

It is the gift of God, given freely. A gift can't be earned.

Not of works, so no one can boast.

If salvation were by works, people could brag about it. "Look what I did! Look how good I was! I earned my way in!"

But salvation is by grace through faith. And that eliminates all boasting.

The only thing anyone contributes to their salvation is the sin that made it necessary.

But What About Works?

Does this mean works don't matter at all? Can people live however they want?

Paul anticipated this question.

Romans 6:1-2

"What shall we say then? Shall we continue in sin, that grace may abound? May it never be! We who died to sin, how could we live in it any longer?"

May it never be! The strongest possible denial.

Those who have truly been saved, truly been transferred from the domain of darkness to the Kingdom of the Son, have died to sin. They're a new creation. They can't just keep living the old way.

Ephesians 2:10

> "For we are his workmanship, created in Christ
> Jesus for good works, which God prepared
> before that we would walk in them."

Good works are not the cause of salvation. They are the result.

We are created in Christ Jesus for good works. Not by good works, for them.

Salvation produces works. Works don't produce salvation.

A fruit tree doesn't become a fruit tree by producing fruit. It produces fruit because it's a fruit tree.

A person doesn't become a Christian by doing good works. They do good works because they've become a Christian.

The order matters. Get it backwards, and the result is the myth of the pearly gates. Get it right, and the result is the gospel.

In Christ

There's a phrase Paul uses over and over, more than 160 times in his letters:

In Christ.

This is the key to everything. Salvation is not just about having sins forgiven. It's about being united with Christ. Joined to Him. In Him.

2 Corinthians 5:17

"Therefore if anyone is in Christ, he is a new creation. The old things have passed away. Behold, all things have become new."

In Christ, a new creation.

Not improved. Not reformed. Not upgraded. New.

The old has passed away. Everything has become new.

This is what happened to the man who believed. In the moment he trusted Christ, he was placed in Christ. He became a new creation. The old, the crime, the guilt, the condemnation, passed away. Everything became new.

He still died on that cross. His body still hung there. But spiritually, everything had changed. He was in Christ. And Christ promised him Paradise.

The Spirit as Guarantee

How does anyone know this is real? How can they know they're truly saved?

God gives a guarantee:

Ephesians 1:13-14

> "In him you also, having heard the word of the truth, the Good News of your salvation, in whom, having also believed, you were sealed with the promised Holy Spirit, who is a pledge of our inheritance, to the redemption of God's own possession, to the praise of his glory."

When someone believes, they are sealed with the Holy Spirit.

Sealed, marked as belonging to God. Secured. Protected.

And the Spirit is a pledge, a down payment, a guarantee, of the inheritance to come.

God doesn't just save people and leave them wondering. He gives His Spirit as proof. The Spirit living in a believer is the guarantee that everything God promised is coming.

Romans 8:16

"The Spirit himself testifies with our spirit that
we are children of God."

The Spirit testifies. He confirms. He assures.

This is not arrogance. This is not presumption. This is
the confidence God wants His children to have.

Those who have trusted Christ have the Spirit. And the
Spirit tells them: You are a child of God.

A Note on Paul's Authority

Some may wonder about Paul. He wasn't one of the original
twelve. He never walked with Jesus during His earthly
ministry. Why should we listen to him?

Because Paul was trained directly by the risen Christ:

Galatians 1:11-12

"For I make known to you, brothers,
concerning the Good News which was
preached by me, that it is not according to
man. For I didn't receive it from man, nor was I
taught it, but it came to me through revelation
of Jesus Christ."

Paul spent time in Arabia, alone with the risen Christ,
receiving the gospel by direct revelation. He didn't get it

secondhand from Peter or James. He got it from Jesus Himself.

And he was given a specific mission:

Romans 11:13

"For I speak to you who are Gentiles. Since then as I am an apostle to Gentiles, I glorify my ministry."

Ephesians 3:8

"To me, the very least of all saints, was this grace given, to preach to the Gentiles the unsearchable riches of Christ."

And the original apostles confirmed his gospel. At the Jerusalem Council (Acts 15), the question was raised: Must Gentiles follow the Law to be saved?

Peter stood and declared:

Acts 15:10-11

"Now therefore why do you tempt God, that you should put a yoke on the neck of the disciples which neither our fathers nor we were able to bear? But we believe that we are saved through the grace of the Lord Jesus, just as they are."

And James, the brother of Jesus and leader of the Jerusalem church, gave the verdict:

Acts 15:19

> "Therefore my judgment is that we don't trouble those from among the Gentiles who turn to God."

Peter said it. James confirmed it. The whole council agreed.

Paul wasn't a rogue teacher inventing his own religion. He was proclaiming the same gospel, revealed to him directly by the risen Christ, and validated by those who walked with Christ before the resurrection. (See Appendix H for a visual timeline of Paul's ministry.)

There is no conflict between Jesus and Paul. The Jerusalem Council settled that in the first century.

Back to the Hill

Look at the man who believed one more time.

He had no works to offer. His hands were nailed to a cross, he couldn't do anything.

He had no religious credentials. He wasn't circumcised that day. He wasn't baptized. He didn't join a church.

He had no time. Hours to live. Maybe minutes.

All he had was faith. Trust in the One dying beside him.

"Lord, remember me when you come into your Kingdom."

And that was enough.

Not because faith is a work that earns salvation. But because faith receives the work that Christ already accomplished.

He trusted Christ. And Christ said: "Today you will be with me in Paradise."

That's justification by faith. Declared righteous. Not by works. Not by effort. Not by being good enough.

By trusting the One who did everything necessary to save him.

* * *

This is the gospel Paul preached. This is the gospel that has saved sinners for two thousand years. This is the gospel that saved the man on the cross, and it's the gospel that can save anyone today.

Not by works, so that no one can boast.

By grace through faith, the gift of God.

Those still trying to earn it will never have peace. They'll always wonder: Have I done enough? Am I good enough?

But those who trust Christ, who stop trying to earn it and simply receive what He offers, can know.

They can know they're forgiven.

They can know they're a new creation.

They can know they have eternal life.

Because it doesn't depend on them. It depends on Him.

And He has already finished the work.

John 19:30

> "When Jesus therefore had received the
> vinegar, he said, 'It is finished.' Then he bowed
> his head and gave up his spirit."

It is finished.

Not "It is started." Not "It is partly done." Not "Now it's your turn."

Finished.

No one's job is to complete what Christ started. The job is to trust what Christ finished.

That's faith. And that's how anyone is made right with God.

The Council at Jerusalem

Acts 15:1

> "Some men came down from Judea and taught
> the brothers, Unless you are circumcised after
> the custom of Moses, you cannot be saved."

Antioch. Approximately 49 AD.

The church is thriving. Gentiles are flooding in,
former pagans, idol worshippers, men and
women who never kept the law of Moses. They
have believed in Jesus. They have been baptized.
They have received the Holy Spirit.

And now men from Judea are telling them it is
not enough.

Unless you are circumcised, you cannot be saved.

The words land like stones. The Gentile believers
look at each other. They thought they were saved.
They thought faith was enough. Now they are
being told there is more, a ritual, a law, a
requirement they knew nothing about.

Acts 15:5

"But some of the sect of the Pharisees who believed rose up, saying, It is necessary to circumcise them, and to command them to keep the law of Moses."

Jerusalem. The council chamber.

Pharisees who have believed in Jesus stand and make their case. They are sincere. They are devout. They are wrong.

It is necessary to circumcise them and command them to keep the law of Moses.

Necessary. That is the word. Not optional. Not recommended. Necessary for salvation.

The room erupts. Voices rise. Arguments fly. Fifteen years of tension between Jewish and Gentile believers come to a head.

And then Peter stands.

Acts 15:7-9

"Brothers, you know that a good while ago God made a choice among you that by my mouth the Gentiles should hear the word of the Good News and believe. God, who knows the heart, testified about them, giving them the Holy Spirit, just as he did to us. He made no distinction between us and them, cleansing their hearts by faith."

The room falls silent. This is Peter. The rock. The one who preached at Pentecost. The one who opened the door to the Gentiles at Cornelius house.

He speaks slowly. Deliberately. Every word weighted with authority.

God made a choice among you that by my mouth the Gentiles should hear the word of the Good News and believe.

Not Peter's choice. God's choice.

God, who knows the heart, testified about them, giving them the Holy Spirit, just as he did to us.

The same Spirit. The same testimony. The same God.

He made no distinction between us and them, cleansing their hearts by faith.

No distinction.

The Pharisees shift uncomfortably. They want to argue. But how do you argue with the Holy Spirit?

Acts 15:10-11

"Now therefore why do you test God, that you should put a yoke on the neck of the disciples which neither our fathers nor we were able to bear? But we believe that we are saved through the grace of the Lord Jesus, just as they are."

Peter's voice rises. His finger points at the Pharisees.

Why do you test God? Why do you put a yoke on the neck of the disciples that neither our fathers nor we were able to bear?

The yoke of the law. Centuries of Israel trying, and failing, to earn what could only be given.

Then Peter delivers the verdict. Simple. Clear. Final.

We believe that we are saved through the grace of the Lord Jesus, just as they are.

Not by circumcision. Not by law-keeping. Not by works.

Grace. Through the Lord Jesus.

The same grace that saved the man on the cross.

Acts 15:19

> "Therefore my judgment is that we do not trouble those from among the Gentiles who turn to God."

James speaks last. The brother of Jesus. The leader of the Jerusalem church. His word will settle the matter.

He quotes the prophet Amos. He traces God's plan from the beginning. And then:

My judgment is that we do not trouble those from among the Gentiles who turn to God.

Do not trouble them. Do not burden them. Do not add to what Christ has already finished.

The gospel remains intact. Faith alone. Grace alone. Christ alone.

This is the gospel the apostles preached.

This is the gospel Paul defended with his life.

This is the gospel he received with his dying breath.

The council confirmed it. The Spirit testified to it. The church has proclaimed it for two thousand years.

Not works. Faith. Not earning. Receiving. Not the law. Grace.

The same Jesus who saved a criminal on a cross can save anyone, Jew or Gentile, slave or free, religious or pagan.

The only requirement is the same one he met: believe.

PART THREE

THE TWO DESTINIES

CHAPTER SIX

What Happens When Believers Die

What happens when a believer dies?

For those who have trusted Christ, this is not a question to fear. Death is not the end, it's a doorway. It's not defeat, it's departure. It's not loss, it's gain.

Let's walk through what Scripture reveals, step by step.

Step One: Immediately with Christ

The moment a believer dies, something wonderful happens. There is no waiting. No soul sleep. No purgatory. No uncertainty.

The believer is immediately with Christ.

2 Corinthians 5:8

> "We are courageous, I say, and are willing rather to be absent from the body and to be at home with the Lord."

> "For to me to live is Christ, and to die is gain.
> But if I live on in the flesh, this will bring fruit
> from my work; yet I don't know what I will
> choose. But I am hard pressed between the
> two, having the desire to depart and be with
> Christ, which is far better."

To die is gain. Far better. Absent from the body, at home with the Lord.

Remember the man on the cross: "Today you will be with me in Paradise." Today. Not eventually. Today.

Step Two: The Intermediate State

This immediate presence with Christ is what theologians call the "intermediate state," the period between death and resurrection.

In this state, the soul is with Christ. The body remains in the grave, awaiting resurrection. The believer is conscious, joyful, at rest, but not yet complete.

This is a wonderful state. Far better than life on earth. But it is not the final state.

Step Three: The Resurrection

When Christ returns, everything changes.

1 Thessalonians 4:16-17

> "For the Lord himself will descend from heaven with a shout, with the voice of the archangel and with God's trumpet. The dead in Christ will rise first, then we who are alive, who are left, will be caught up together with them in the clouds to meet the Lord in the air. So we will be with the Lord forever."

1 Corinthians 15:51-54

> "Behold, I tell you a mystery. We will not all sleep, but we will all be changed, in a moment, in the twinkling of an eye, at the last trumpet. For the trumpet will sound and the dead will be raised incorruptible, and we will be changed. For this perishable body must become imperishable, and this mortal must put on immortality. But when this perishable body will have become imperishable, and this mortal will have put on immortality, then what is written will happen: 'Death is swallowed up in victory.'"

Bodies raised. Transformed. Imperishable. Immortal. Death swallowed up in victory.

Step Four: The Judgment Seat of Christ

After resurrection comes judgment. But for the believer, this is not a judgment of condemnation.

Romans 8:1

"There is therefore now no condemnation to those who are in Christ Jesus."

2 Corinthians 5:10

"For we must all be made manifest before the judgment seat of Christ, that each one may receive the things in the body according to what he has done, whether good or bad."

This is about rewards, what the believer did with their life after they were saved. Not about whether they get in. That's already settled by faith.

Step Five: Reigning with Christ

Revelation 20:6

"Blessed and holy is he who has part in the first resurrection. Over these, the second death has no power, but they will be priests of God and of Christ, and will reign with him one thousand years."

Believers will reign. Priests and kings. Not passive existence, active, purposeful life forever.

Step Six: The New Heaven and New Earth

Revelation 21:1-4

"I saw a new heaven and a new earth, for the first heaven and the first earth have passed away, and the sea is no more. I saw the holy city, New Jerusalem, coming down out of heaven from God, prepared like a bride adorned for her husband. I heard a loud voice out of heaven saying, 'Behold, God's dwelling is with people; and he will dwell with them, and they will be his people, and God himself will be with them as their God. He will wipe away every tear from their eyes. Death will be no more; neither will there be mourning, nor crying, nor pain any more. The first things have passed away.'"

God dwelling with His people. No more tears. No more death. Forever.

Back to the Hill

The man who believed heard: "Today you will be with me in Paradise." That very day, his soul was with Jesus. When Christ returns, his body will be raised. He will reign with Christ forever. A criminal turned king. All because of the middle cross.

John 11:25-26

> "Jesus said to her, 'I am the resurrection and the life. He who believes in me will still live, even if he dies. Whoever lives and believes in me will never die. Do you believe this?'"

"Do you believe this?" That's the question Jesus asked Martha. It's the question that determines everything.

Today

Luke 23:43

> "Jesus said to him, Assuredly, I tell you, today you will be with me in Paradise."

Today.

The word echoes in the criminal's mind as his lungs finally give out. The weight of his body has become too much. The muscles that lift his chest have failed. The darkness that covered the land is now covering his eyes.

Today.

He heard the promise. He believed the promise. And now...

---

2 Corinthians 5:8

"We are courageous, I say, and are willing rather to be absent from the body and to be at home with the Lord."

The pain is gone.

That is the first thing he notices. The fire in his wrists, gone. The crushing weight on his chest, gone. The slow suffocation that had been drowning him for hours, gone.

He takes a breath. A real breath. Full and deep and free.

He opens his eyes.

He is not on the cross.

He is standing. His legs, the same legs the soldiers were preparing to break, are whole. His hands, the same hands that were pinned to rough wood, are unmarked.

No blood. No wounds. No scars.

He looks at himself. He is the same man. But different. Restored. Complete.

Absent from the body. At home with the Lord.

Revelation 22:4

> "They will see his face, and his name will be on their foreheads."

The Man from the middle cross.

But He is not dying now. He is not gasping for breath. He is not wearing a crown of thorns.

He is radiant. He is glorious. He is smiling.

He sees His face. The same face he saw through blood and sweat and tears on Golgotha. The same face that turned to him and spoke Paradise.

Welcome.

Ephesians 2:8-9

"For by grace you have been saved through faith, and that not of yourselves; it is the gift of God, not of works, that no one would boast."

Lord, he whispers, I do not understand. I was a criminal. I was guilty. I deserved that cross.

Jesus steps forward. He takes his hands, the same hands that once stole, that once were nailed beside Him.

Yes. You did.

Then how...?

By grace you have been saved. Through faith. Not of yourself. It is the gift of God.

He stares at his hands. Clean. Unmarked. Forgiven.

I had nothing to offer.

You had faith. It was enough.

John 14:3

"If I go and prepare a place for you, I will come again and will receive you to myself; that where I am, you may be also."

Come, Jesus says. There is much to see. I have prepared a place for you.

He walks beside the King. The same King who hung beside him on a Roman cross. The same King who spoke Paradise over him while the crowd mocked.

He still does not fully understand. He may never fully understand.

But he is here. He is whole. He is home.

Where Jesus is, he is also.

Today.

This is what awaits every believer.

Not a distant hope. Not a someday promise. Today.

Absent from the body. Present with the Lord.

He was the first fruit of the cross. The first soul redeemed by the blood that was still wet on the wood.

He will not be the last.

Everyone who trusts in Christ, whether on a cross or in a hospital bed, whether with decades of service or seconds of faith, will open their eyes and see the same face.

The face of the One who remembered them.

CHAPTER SEVEN

What Happens When Unbelievers Die

This is a difficult chapter to write. But the Bible is clear. And if the truth is to be told, the whole truth, this cannot be skipped.

What happens to those who die without Christ?

Jesus Himself gave us the clearest picture. It's a story that should make every person stop and think.

The Rich Man and Lazarus

In Luke 16, Jesus tells of two men. Their lives could not have been more different. And neither could their deaths.

Luke 16:19-21

> "Now there was a certain rich man, and he was
> clothed in purple and fine linen, living in
> luxury every day. A certain beggar, named
> Lazarus, was taken to his gate, full of sores,
> and desiring to be fed with the crumbs that fell

from the rich man's table. Yes, even the dogs
came and licked his sores."

The rich man had everything. Fine clothes. Daily luxury. A gate, meaning a large estate. He lived well.

Lazarus had nothing. He was laid at the gate, too weak to get there himself. Covered in sores. So destitute he longed for scraps from the rich man's table. Even the dogs came to lick his wounds.

By any worldly measure, the rich man was blessed and Lazarus was cursed.

Then they died.

Immediately to Their Destinations

Luke 16:22-23

"The beggar died, and he was carried away by the angels to Abraham's bosom. The rich man also died and was buried. In Hades, he lifted up his eyes, being in torment, and saw Abraham far off, and Lazarus at his bosom."

Notice what happened immediately.

Lazarus died and was carried by angels to Abraham's bosom, a place of comfort, rest, and fellowship with the patriarch of faith.

The rich man died and was buried. His body was probably given an elaborate funeral. But his soul went to Hades, and he lifted up his eyes in torment.

No delay. No waiting room. No purgatory. No soul sleep. Immediate destination based on their standing before God.

Conscious Awareness

What is Hades like? Jesus tells us.

Luke 16:24

> "He cried and said, 'Father Abraham, have
> mercy on me, and send Lazarus, that he may
> dip the tip of his finger in water and cool my
> tongue! For I am in anguish in this flame.'"

The rich man could see. He saw Abraham far off. He saw Lazarus.

He could speak. He cried out, begging for mercy.

He could feel. He was in anguish, tormented by flame, desperate for even a drop of water on his tongue.

He could remember. He knew who Lazarus was. He remembered his life, his brothers, his choices.

This is not unconsciousness. This is not annihilation. This is conscious, aware, agonizing existence.

And it had only just begun.

Memory and Regret

Perhaps the cruelest aspect of Hades is memory.

Luke 16:25

> "But Abraham said, 'Son, remember that you,
> in your lifetime, received your good things,
> and Lazarus, in the same way, bad things. But
> now here he is comforted and you are in
> anguish.'"

Remember. The rich man could recall every luxury, every feast, every day he walked past Lazarus at his gate and did nothing. Every sermon he heard and ignored. Every opportunity he wasted.

In Hades, there is no forgetting. No distraction. No numbing the pain. Just endless memory of what was and what could have been.

The man who scoffed will remember the middle cross forever. He will remember every word Jesus spoke. He will remember the other man who believed. He will remember his own mockery. And he will never be able to undo it.

The Great Chasm

Luke 16:26

> "Besides all this, between us and you there is a
> great gulf fixed, that those who want to pass
> from here to you are not able, and that no one
> may cross over from there to us."

A great gulf fixed. Not a gap that might be bridged. Not a distance that could be crossed with enough effort. Fixed. Permanent. Impassable.

Those in comfort cannot go to those in torment, even if they wanted to.

Those in torment cannot escape to comfort, no matter how desperately they try.

The rich man asked for mercy. He received truth instead: it's too late.

This is the weight of the gospel. The door is open now. But it will not be open forever. Once death comes, the chasm is fixed. No crossing. No second chances. No appeals.

Concern for the Living

What happened next reveals something important about those in Hades.

Luke 16:27-28

> "He said, 'I ask you therefore, father, that you would send him to my father's house, for I have five brothers, that he may testify to them, so they won't also come into this place of torment.'"

The rich man had five brothers still living. Still on the other side of death. Still with a chance.

He begged Abraham to send Lazarus back from the dead to warn them. If someone came back from the grave, surely they would listen. Surely they would repent.

Notice: even in torment, he still thought he could give orders to Lazarus. Old habits die hard. But more importantly, notice his desperation. He knew what was coming for his brothers if they continued on their path.

This is what those in Hades would say to the living if they could speak: Don't come here. Turn around. Believe while you still can.

The Scriptures Are Enough

Luke 16:29-31

> "But Abraham said, 'They have Moses and the
> prophets. Let them listen to them.' He said,
> 'No, father Abraham, but if one goes to them
> from the dead, they will repent.' He said to
> him, 'If they don't listen to Moses and the
> prophets, neither will they be persuaded if one
> rises from the dead.'"

Abraham's answer is sobering.

They have Moses and the prophets. They have
Scripture. They have the Word of God. That should be
enough.

The rich man disagreed. If someone rose from the
dead, that would convince them!

But Abraham knew better. If they won't believe the
Scriptures, they won't believe even if someone rises from the
dead.

And Someone did rise from the dead. Jesus Christ. And
still people refuse to believe.

The problem is not lack of evidence. The problem is
hardness of heart.

This is why the message of Scripture matters. This is why "faith comes by hearing, and hearing by the word of God" (Romans 10:17). The Scriptures are sufficient. Those who reject them will reject anything.

The Great White Throne

Hades is not the final destination. It is the waiting place.

Those who die without Christ go to Hades immediately. But they remain there only until the final judgment.

Revelation 20:11-15

"I saw a great white throne and him who sat on it, from whose face the earth and the heaven fled away. There was found no place for them. I saw the dead, the great and the small, standing before the throne, and books were opened. Another book was opened, which is the book of life. The dead were judged out of the things which were written in the books, according to their works. The sea gave up the dead who were in it. Death and Hades gave up the dead who were in them. They were judged, each one according to his works. Death and Hades were thrown into the lake of fire. This is the second death, the lake of fire. If anyone was not found written in the book of life, he was

cast into the lake of fire."

Hades gives up its dead. They are resurrected, but not to life. They are resurrected to stand before the Great White Throne.

Books are opened, a record of every deed. And another book, the Book of Life.

If their name is not in the Book of Life, the verdict is final: the lake of fire. The second death.

The Lake of Fire

Matthew 25:41

"Then he will say also to those on the left hand,

'Depart from me, you cursed, into the eternal

fire which is prepared for the devil and his

angels.'"

The lake of fire was prepared for the devil and his angels. It was never meant for human beings. But those who follow Satan, whether knowingly or not, will share his fate.

Matthew 25:46

"These will go away into eternal punishment,

but the righteous into eternal life."

Eternal punishment. The same word used for eternal life. If heaven is forever, hell is forever.

This is not written to condemn, but to warn. This is where the road leads without Christ. This is what the gospel rescues people from.

God takes no pleasure in the death of the wicked (Ezekiel 33:11). He is patient, not wanting anyone to perish (2 Peter 3:9). But He will not force anyone into His Kingdom. Those who choose darkness will have darkness, forever.

Back to the Hill

The man who scoffed heard silence from Jesus. No promise. No Paradise. He died on that cross and went to Hades.

He is there still, waiting for the final judgment. Remembering the chance he had. Remembering the words he spoke. Remembering the One who hung beside him and offered salvation to anyone who would believe.

He had the same opportunity as the other man. The same proximity. The same invitation.

But he scoffed. And scoffing, he died. And dying, he entered torment. And there, he waits.

Hebrews 9:27

"Inasmuch as it is appointed for men to die once, and after this, judgment."

After death, judgment. But before death, grace. The door is still open.

The rich man's brothers still had time. So does everyone reading this. The question is what they will do with it.

The Silence

Luke 23:39

"One of the criminals who was hanged insulted him, saying, If you are the Christ, save yourself and us!"

The man on the left cross is still alive.

His lungs are failing. His arms have gone numb. Every breath is a battle against the weight of his own body. But he is still conscious. Still watching. Still refusing.

He hurled his demands at the man in the middle. If you are the Christ, save yourself and us!

If. Prove it. Do something. Get me off this cross.

The man in the middle said nothing back.

Luke 23:44-45

"It was now about the sixth hour, and darkness came over the whole land until the ninth hour. The sun was darkened..."

And then the sky goes dark.

It is noon. The sun should be at its peak. But darkness rolls over Jerusalem like a blanket thrown over a lamp. Not clouds. Not an eclipse. Something else. Something unnatural.

The crowd falls silent. Even the mockers stop mocking.

For three hours, darkness covers the land.

The man on the left hangs in the blackness. He can hear the man in the middle breathing, labored, ragged, fading. He can hear the other criminal gasping for air. But he cannot see them.

Three hours of darkness. Three hours to think.
Three hours to change his mind.

He does not.

Matthew 27:51

"Behold, the veil of the temple was torn in two
from the top to the bottom. The earth quaked
and the rocks were split."

What happens next will haunt the scoffing
criminal for eternity.

The earth shakes.

Not a tremor. A violent, rolling earthquake that
splits rocks and tears open the ground. The
crosses sway. The soldiers stumble. The crowd
screams and scatters.

And from the city, from the temple itself, word
begins to spread.

The veil is torn.

The curtain that separates the Holy Place from the
Most Holy Place, sixty feet tall, four inches thick,

the barrier between God and man, has been ripped in two.

From top to bottom.

Not torn by human hands. Torn by God Himself.

Matthew 27:52-54

"The tombs were opened, and many bodies of the saints who had fallen asleep were raised; and coming out of the tombs after his resurrection, they entered into the holy city and appeared to many. Now the centurion and those who were with him watching Jesus, when they saw the earthquake and the things that were done, feared exceedingly, saying, Truly this was the Son of God."

And there is more.

Tombs are opening. The dead are rising. The bodies of saints who died in faith, Abraham's children, men and women who waited for the Messiah, are walking out of their graves.

They will enter Jerusalem. They will be seen by many. The dead are walking while the man on the left cross is still dying.

He sees none of this. He is still on the hill. But he hears the reports. He feels the earthquake. He hangs in the aftermath of something cosmic.

And still he does not believe.

The centurion, a Roman soldier, a pagan, a man who has crucified hundreds, falls to his knees.

Truly this was the Son of God.

A Roman sees it. A man who worships Caesar and Jupiter and Mars looks at the dead body of Jesus and recognizes deity.

The religious leaders refuse to see it. They will go home and wash their hands and prepare for the Sabbath.

And the man on the left cross?

He saw the darkness. He felt the earthquake. He heard the centurion's confession.

He is hanging within arm's reach of the torn veil, the split rocks, the opened tombs.

And still he demands works instead of offering faith.

Luke 16:23-24

"In Hades, he lifted up his eyes, being in torment, and saw Abraham far off, and Lazarus at his bosom. He cried and said, Father Abraham, have mercy on me, and send Lazarus, that he may dip the tip of his finger in water and cool my tongue! For I am in anguish in this flame."

The man on the left takes his final breath.

His body sags. His eyes close.

And he opens them in darkness.

Not the darkness of Golgotha. Something different. Something permanent. Something worse.

He can see now, but he wishes he could not.

He can feel, but what he feels is torment.

He can remember, but every memory is a knife.

Anguish. Flame. Thirst that will never be quenched.

The man who demanded rescue from the cross now begs for a single drop of water.

But there is no water here. No relief. No rescue.

Luke 16:26

> "Besides all this, between us and you there is a great gulf fixed, that those who want to pass from here to you are not able, and that no one may cross over from there to us."

A great gulf. Fixed. Permanent. Impassable.

No crossing over. No second chance. No appeal.

The man who hung on the right side of Jesus is in Paradise, today, just as promised.

The man who hung on the left side of Jesus is in torment, forever, just as warned.

Same hill. Same hour. Same opportunity. Same Savior within arm's reach.

The only difference was a decision.

This is where the road leads without Christ.

Not annihilation. Not soul sleep. Not a second chance.

Conscious torment. Permanent separation. Eternal regret.

The door was open on that hill. The same door that let the man who believed into Paradise could have let the man who scoffed in too.

But he demanded proof instead of offering faith.

The door is still open today. But it will not be forever.

CHAPTER EIGHT

The Timeline

Where is history headed? The Bible tells us. (See Appendix I for a visual timeline of biblical history.)

The Return of Christ

Acts 1:11

> "...who also said, 'You men of Galilee, why do you stand looking into the sky? This Jesus, who was received up from you into the sky, will come back in the same way as you saw him going into the sky.'"

He's coming back. The same Jesus. Visibly, bodily, gloriously.

The Rapture

1 Thessalonians 4:16-17

> "For the Lord himself will descend from heaven with a shout, with the voice of the

archangel and with God's trumpet. The dead in Christ will rise first, then we who are alive, who are left, will be caught up together with them in the clouds to meet the Lord in the air. So we will be with the Lord forever."

The dead rise. The living are changed. All believers gathered to Christ.

The Millennium

Revelation 20:6

"Blessed and holy is he who has part in the first resurrection. Over these, the second death has no power, but they will be priests of God and of Christ, and will reign with him one thousand years."

Christ reigning on earth. Believers reigning with Him. Priests and kings.

Satan's End

Revelation 20:10

"The devil who deceived them was thrown into the lake of fire and sulfur, where the beast and

the false prophet are also. They will be
tormented day and night forever and ever."

Satan's final end. The lake of fire. Forever.

The New Heaven and New Earth

Revelation 21:5

"He who sits on the throne said, 'Behold, I am
making all things new.'"

This is where history is headed: Christ wins. Satan loses.
Death is destroyed. God dwells with His people. Forever.

Everything on this timeline flows from what happened
on that hill outside Jerusalem. The cross was the decisive
battle. Everything since has been the outworking of that
victory. Everything ahead will be its completion. (See
Appendix I for a visual overview of God's prophetic
timeline.)

Heaven Opened

Acts 7:54-56

"Now when they heard these things, they were
cut to the heart, and they gnashed at him with
their teeth. But he, being full of the Holy Spirit,
looked up steadfastly into heaven and saw the

glory of God, and Jesus standing on the right hand of God, and said, Behold, I see the heavens opened and the Son of Man standing at the right hand of God!"

Jerusalem. Approximately 34 AD.

The Sanhedrin is in an uproar. The same council that condemned Jesus is now facing one of His followers, a man named Stephen, full of faith and the Holy Spirit.

Stephen has just finished speaking. He has traced the history of Israel from Abraham to Moses to Solomon to the prophets. He has shown them their pattern: resisting the Holy Spirit, persecuting the prophets, betraying and murdering the Righteous One.

They are grinding their teeth. They are covering their ears. They do not want to hear another word.

But Stephen is no longer looking at them.

Stephen looks up.

His face changes. The witnesses will later say it looked like the face of an angel. Something is happening that the Sanhedrin cannot see.

Behold, I see the heavens opened!

The council freezes. Opened? The heavens?

And the Son of Man standing at the right hand of God!

Standing. Not sitting. Not resting on His throne.

Jesus Christ, the same Jesus they condemned, the same Jesus they crucified, the same Jesus they thought they had silenced forever, is alive. And He is standing.

Standing to receive His servant.

Acts 7:58-59

"They threw him out of the city and stoned him. The witnesses placed their garments at the feet of a young man named Saul. They stoned Stephen as he called out, saying, Lord Jesus, receive my spirit!"

A young man stands nearby. His name is Saul. He is a Pharisee, trained under Gamaliel, zealous for the traditions of his fathers.

He holds the coats of the executioners. He approves of this. Stephen is a blasphemer, a heretic, a danger to the faith of Israel.

Saul is wrong. But he does not know it yet.

He watches as the stones begin to fly.

The stones strike Stephen's head, his shoulders, his back. Blood pours. Bones crack.

But Stephen does not curse. Stephen does not beg.

He calls out, not to the council, not to the crowd, but to the One he sees standing in heaven.

Lord Jesus, receive my spirit!

The same words Jesus spoke on the cross: Father, into your hands I commit my spirit.

Stephen is following his Lord. All the way to death.

Acts 7:60

"He kneeled down and cried with a loud voice, Lord, do not hold this sin against them! When he had said this, he fell asleep."

Stephen falls to his knees. The stones keep coming. His vision blurs. But he can still see heaven. He can still see Jesus standing.

One more breath. One more prayer.

Lord, do not hold this sin against them!

The same prayer Jesus prayed on the cross: Father, forgive them, for they do not know what they are doing.

And then Stephen is gone.

He fell asleep.

That is how Scripture describes the death of a believer. Not extinction. Not annihilation. Sleep. The body rests while the spirit goes home.

Stephen's body lies in the pit. Broken. Bloody. Still.

But Stephen? Stephen is with Jesus.

The same Jesus he saw standing. The same Jesus who received his spirit. The same Jesus who welcomed the man who believed into Paradise just a few years earlier.

Stephen opened his eyes and saw no more stones. No more blood. No more Sanhedrin.

Just the face of Christ.

Home.

Acts 9:3-5

"As he traveled, he got close to Damascus, and suddenly a light from the sky shone around him. He fell on the earth and heard a voice saying to him, Saul, Saul, why do you persecute me? He said, Who are you, Lord? The Lord said, I am Jesus, whom you are persecuting."

Saul walks away that day, coats in hand, convinced he has served God.

But he will remember Stephen's face. The peace. The glow. The prayer for forgiveness.

It will haunt him until the Damascus road.

The same Jesus Stephen saw standing will knock Saul to the ground.

The same voice that spoke Paradise to the man who believed will speak Saul's name on the Damascus road.

Saul, Saul, why do you persecute me?

Who are you, Lord?

I am Jesus.

The man who held the coats will become the apostle who writes half the New Testament. The man who consented to Stephen's death will suffer beatings, shipwrecks, stonings, and chains for the name he once tried to destroy.

Because he finally saw what Stephen saw: Jesus is alive. Jesus is standing. Jesus is Lord.

This is what awaits believers.

Not a cold, silent grave. Not an uncertain void.

A risen Savior. Standing. Waiting. Ready to receive.

Stephen saw it. He experienced it. Every believer who has died since has found the same thing.

Absent from the body. Present with the Lord.

The heavens are still open. The Son of Man is still standing. The invitation is still offered.

PART FOUR

WHY YOU'RE STILL HERE

CHAPTER NINE

Ambassadors Behind Enemy Lines

Those who have trusted Christ have been transferred. Delivered from the domain of darkness. Translated into the Kingdom of the Son.

So why are they still here?

The answer is simple: There is a mission.

Citizens of Heaven

Philippians 3:20

"For our citizenship is in heaven, from which we also wait for a Savior, the Lord Jesus Christ."

1 Peter 2:11

"Beloved, I beg you as foreigners and pilgrims, to abstain from fleshly lusts which war against the soul."

Citizenship in heaven. Foreigners here. Pilgrims passing through.

Ambassadors for Christ

2 Corinthians 5:20

> "We are therefore ambassadors for Christ, as though God were making his appeal through us. We beg you on behalf of Christ, be reconciled to God."

An ambassador represents one nation to another. Lives in a foreign country, but speaks for the home country. Carries the message of the king.

God makes His appeal through His people. When they share the gospel, it's not just them talking. It's God appealing through them.

The Ministry of Reconciliation

2 Corinthians 5:18-19

> "But all things are of God, who reconciled us to himself through Jesus Christ, and gave to us the ministry of reconciliation; namely, that God was in Christ reconciling the world to himself, not reckoning to them their trespasses, and

having committed to us the word of reconciliation."

God reconciled us to Himself, and then gave us the ministry of reconciliation. The message is: Reconciliation is possible. The war can end. The separation can be healed. Come home.

The Great Commission

Matthew 28:19-20

"Go and make disciples of all nations, baptizing them in the name of the Father and of the Son and of the Holy Spirit, teaching them to observe all things that I commanded you. Behold, I am with you always, even to the end of the age."

Behind Enemy Lines

Ephesians 6:12

"For our wrestling is not against flesh and blood, but against the principalities, against the powers, against the world's rulers of the darkness of this age, and against the spiritual forces of wickedness in the heavenly places."

This is enemy territory. The battle is not against people. Unbelievers are not enemies to fight, they are captives to rescue.

Someone once told each believer the gospel. Someone was an ambassador to them. Someone carried the message that set them free.

Now it's their turn.

Back to the Hill

The man who believed didn't have time for mission. He trusted Christ and went to Paradise that very day.

But most believers have time. Days, weeks, years, perhaps decades.

The rich man begged for someone to warn his brothers. He couldn't go. The dead cannot return.

But the living can speak. The living can warn. The living can carry the message.

That's why believers are still here.

The Scars on His Back

2 Corinthians 11:24-25

"Five times I received forty stripes minus one from the Jews. Three times I was beaten with rods. Once I was stoned. Three times I suffered shipwreck. I have been a night and a day in the deep."

Somewhere in the Roman Empire. A prison cell. Night.

The apostle Paul sits against a cold stone wall. His back is a map of scars.

Forty stripes minus one. That is thirty-nine lashes. Five times.

One hundred ninety-five strokes of a whip embedded with bone and metal, designed to tear flesh from muscle.

Most men do not survive one beating. Paul survived five.

---

2 Corinthians 11:26-27

"I have been in travels often, perils of rivers, perils of robbers, perils from my countrymen, perils from the Gentiles, perils in the city, perils in the wilderness, perils in the sea, perils among false brothers; in labor and travail, in watchings often, in hunger and thirst, in fastings often, and in cold and nakedness."

Paul runs his fingers across the raised welts on his back. Each scar is a city. Each wound is a church planted.

Philippi, beaten with rods, thrown into prison.

Lystra, stoned and left for dead.

Corinth, dragged before the judgment seat.

Jerusalem, arrested, bound, nearly torn apart by a mob.

Why did he not stop? Why did he not stay silent?

One word, I recant, and the beatings would have ended. One compromise, Caesar is Lord, and he could have gone free.

But Paul saw something the Romans could not see.

---

2 Corinthians 12:2-4

"I know a man in Christ, fourteen years ago (whether in the body, I do not know, or whether out of the body, I do not know; God knows), such a one was caught up into the third heaven. I know such a man (whether in the body, or outside of the body, I do not know; God knows), how he was caught up into Paradise and heard unspeakable words, which it is not lawful for a man to utter."

Paul was caught up to Paradise. The third heaven. The very presence of God.

He heard things no human tongue can repeat. He saw what awaits those who trust Christ. He glimpsed the glory that outweighs every affliction.

That is why he endures.

He has seen the end of the story. He knows how it finishes. And one hundred ninety-five lashes are nothing compared to eternity.

Romans 8:18

"For I consider that the sufferings of this present time are not worthy to be compared with the glory which will be revealed toward us."

Paul picks up a reed pen. The parchment before him will become a letter, to Rome, to Corinth, to Ephesus, to Timothy.

His hands shake. The cold. The hunger. The wounds that never fully heal.

But he writes.

The sufferings of this present time are not worthy to be compared...

He means it. He has calculated it. One hundred ninety-five lashes against eternal glory. Stonings and shipwrecks against a crown that will never fade.

The math is clear.

"For I am persuaded that neither death, nor
life, nor angels, nor principalities, nor things
present, nor things to come, nor powers, nor
height, nor depth, nor any other created thing
will be able to separate us from God's love
which is in Christ Jesus our Lord."

Paul writes the words that will echo through
centuries.

For I am persuaded...

Persuaded. Convinced. Certain beyond all doubt.

...that neither death, nor life, nor angels, nor
principalities, nor things present, nor things to
come, nor powers, nor height, nor depth, nor any
other created thing will be able to separate us
from God's love which is in Christ Jesus our Lord.

He has tested it. Death has tried to separate him
from Christ, one hundred ninety-five times across
his back, plus stonings, shipwrecks, a night and a
day in the deep.

None of it worked.

Nothing can separate him from the love of God in Christ Jesus.

Nothing.

Philippians 1:21

"For to me, to live is Christ and to die is gain."

In another cell, another prisoner watches. A guard, perhaps, or a fellow inmate. He has seen the scars. He has heard Paul singing hymns at midnight. He has watched this broken old man write letters as if the fate of the world depended on them.

Why? he finally asks. Why do you keep going?

Paul looks up. His eyes, once blinded on the Damascus road, now seeing more clearly than most, fix on the man.

For to me, to live is Christ and to die is gain.

If I live, I serve Christ. If I die, I go to Christ. Either way, I win.

The man stares. He does not understand. Not yet.

"For I am already being poured out, and the time of my departure has come. I have fought the good fight. I have finished the course. I have kept the faith. From now on, the crown of righteousness is stored up for me, which the Lord, the righteous judge, will give to me on that day; and not to me only, but also to all those who have loved his appearing."

Paul returns to his letter. His final letter. The time of his departure has come.

I have fought the good fight. I have finished the course. I have kept the faith.

The scars on his back are not wounds. They are receipts.

Every lash paid for a soul who heard the gospel and believed. Every beating purchased another church, another convert, another name written in the Book of Life.

From now on, the crown of righteousness is stored up for me.

He knows what is coming. Not just death, departure. Not just an ending, a beginning.

The same Paradise he glimpsed years ago. The same Christ who knocked him off his horse. The same promise spoken to a dying man.

Today, you will be with me.

This is why believers remain on earth.

Not to be comfortable. Not to be safe. Not to blend in.

But to testify. To reconcile. To beg on behalf of Christ: be reconciled to God.

Paul understood it. The scars proved it.

The same Christ who hung on a cross between two criminals called Paul to carry the message to the ends of the earth.

The same gospel that saved a dying man can save anyone, if someone is willing to tell them.

That is why we are still here.

The ministry of reconciliation. The message of the cross. The invitation that is still open.

Are we willing to bear the scars?

CHAPTER TEN

The Urgency of Now

The door is open. But it won't be open forever.

The Rich Man's Regret

Luke 16:27-28

> "He said, 'I ask you therefore, father, that you
> would send him to my father's house, for I
> have five brothers, that he may testify to them,
> so they won't also come into this place of
> torment.'"

Five brothers still alive. Still on the other side of death. Still with a chance.

"Please. Warn them. So they won't come here."

This is the cry of everyone in Hades. If they could speak to the living, this is what they would say: Don't come here. Turn around. Believe while you still can.

But they can't speak to the living. The door is closed. The only ones who can warn the living are the living.

Why God Waits

2 Peter 3:9

> "The Lord is not slow concerning his promise,
> as some count slowness; but he is patient
> toward us, not wishing that anyone should
> perish, but that all should come to repentance."

God is patient. He doesn't want anyone to perish. Every day that passes is another opportunity for people to repent.

But the patience has a limit. The window has a closing time.

Today Is the Day

2 Corinthians 6:2

> "For he says, 'At an acceptable time I listened
> to you. In a day of salvation I helped you.'
> Behold, now is the acceptable time. Behold,
> now is the day of salvation."

Hebrews 3:15

> "...while it is said, 'Today if you will hear his
> voice, don't harden your hearts...'"

Today, today, today. The Bible keeps repeating it because people keep forgetting it.

The Danger of Delay

Earlier we saw the terrifying progression in Romans 1. Those who continue to reject God are given over, to uncleanness, to vile passions, to a debased mind.

This is why delay is so dangerous. It's not just that death could come unexpectedly. It's that the heart can become so hardened, so darkened, that it loses the ability to respond.

Pharaoh hardened his heart. And eventually, God hardened it further. There came a point of no return.

No one knows where that point is. No one should presume they can wait until tomorrow. The door is open now. Tomorrow is not guaranteed.

Isaiah 55:6

> "Seek Yahweh while he may be found. Call on
> him while he is near."

While He may be found. While He is near.

The implication is sobering: There will come a time when He may not be found. When seeking Him will be too late.

Now is not that time.

Now He can be found.

Now He is near.

Now is the day of salvation.

The Brevity of Life

James 4:14

"...whereas you don't know what your life will
be like tomorrow. For what is your life? For
you are a vapor that appears for a little time
and then vanishes away."

Life is vapor. A mist. Here for a moment, then gone.

The man who believed had hours. Maybe minutes. He
didn't have the luxury of putting it off.

No one knows how much time they have.

Back to the Hill

Two men. One moment.

The man who believed seized the moment. With his
dying breath, he trusted Christ.

The man who scoffed let the moment pass. He could
have believed. He heard the same words. He saw the same
Savior. But he wasted his final breaths on mockery.

And then it was too late.

The window closed. The door shut. The chasm became fixed.

Both thieves ran out of time. But only one used the time he had.

What Must I Do?

Acts 16:22-24

> "The multitude rose up together against them;
> and the magistrates tore their clothes off them,
> and commanded them to be beaten with rods.
> When they had laid many stripes on them,
> they threw them into prison, charging the jailer
> to keep them safely. Having received such a
> command, he threw them into the inner prison
> and fastened their feet in the stocks."

Philippi. Approximately 50 AD.

Paul and Silas are thrown into the inner cell. The deepest part of the prison. The darkest. The most secure.

Their backs are shredded from the beating, many stripes, Luke writes. Their wrists are raw from the ropes. Their feet are locked in wooden stocks, stretched apart, unable to move.

The jailer checks the locks one final time. These two Jews are not going anywhere.

He should feel satisfied. The prisoners are secure. Roman justice is intact.

But something is about to happen that will shatter his world.

Acts 16:25

> "But about midnight Paul and Silas were praying and singing hymns to God, and the prisoners were listening to them."

Midnight.

The jailer cannot sleep. Something is wrong. Something is different.

The Jews are singing.

Their backs are torn open. Their feet are fastened in stocks. They have not eaten. They have not slept. They should be moaning, cursing, begging for water.

Instead, they are singing hymns.

The other prisoners are awake, listening. No one has ever heard anything like this. What kind of men sing after a beating like that?

Acts 16:26

"Suddenly there was a great earthquake, so that the foundations of the prison were shaken; and immediately all the doors were opened, and everyone's bonds were loosened."

And then the earthquake hits.

Not a tremor. A great earthquake. The foundations of the prison shake. The walls crack. The jailer is thrown from his bed.

And then, the sound of iron crashing. Wood snapping. Chains falling.

The doors are open. Every door. The stocks are broken. Every stock. The chains are loose. Every chain.

The prisoners are free.

Acts 16:27-28

"The jailer, being roused out of sleep and seeing the prison doors open, drew his sword and was about to kill himself, supposing that the prisoners had escaped. But Paul cried with a loud voice, saying, Do not harm yourself, for we are all here!"

The jailer scrambles to his feet. He grabs a torch. He sees what he feared most.

Every door open. Every chain broken.

Roman law is clear. If a prisoner escapes, the jailer pays with his life. Public execution. Slow. Painful. Humiliating.

Better to die by his own sword.

He draws the blade. He raises it to his chest.

A voice echoes from the darkness.

Do not harm yourself! We are all here!

The jailer freezes. He peers into the inner cell. The torch light flickers across the walls.

Paul and Silas are still there. Stocks shattered. Chains on the ground. Free to run.

But they stayed.

All the prisoners stayed.

Acts 16:29-30

"He called for lights, and sprang in, and fell down trembling before Paul and Silas, and brought them out and said, Sirs, what must I do to be saved?"

The jailer calls for more torches. He rushes into the inner cell. He falls at their feet, the same prisoners he locked up hours ago.

His hands are trembling. His voice is breaking.

Sirs, what must I do to be saved?

He is not asking how to keep his job. He is not asking how to avoid Roman punishment.

He has seen something. Felt something. Heard something.

These men have a peace he does not have. A joy he does not have. A God who sends earthquakes to break chains and opens doors without unlocking them.

What must I do to be saved?

It is the only question that matters.

Acts 16:31

"They said, Believe in the Lord Jesus Christ, and you will be saved, you and your house."

Paul's answer is immediate. No hesitation. No lengthy explanation. No list of requirements.

Believe in the Lord Jesus Christ, and you will be saved.

Believe.

Not be circumcised. Not follow the law. Not clean up your life first. Not prove yourself worthy.

Believe.

The same word Jesus spoke to the man on the cross. The same faith that opened Paradise. The same gospel that Paul had been beaten for preaching.

One word. One requirement. One Savior.

Believe.

Acts 16:33-34

"He took them the same hour of the night and washed their stripes, and was immediately baptized, he and all his household. He brought them up into his house and set food before them, and rejoiced greatly with all his household, having believed in God."

That night, Paul and Silas speak the word of the Lord to the jailer and his entire household. Servants. Family. Children. Everyone hears the gospel.

That night, the jailer, the same man who locked them in stocks, washes their wounds. His hands, calloused from chains and keys, gently clean the blood from their backs.

That night, the jailer and his entire household are baptized. The same prison that held Paul and Silas now witnesses their converts' public declaration of faith.

Everything changed in one night. One earthquake. One question. One decision.

The jailer sets a table. The men who were beaten and chained now eat as honored guests. The household rejoices together.

Having believed in God.

That is all it took. Faith. Trust. Surrender.

The same faith he showed on the cross.

The same faith that has saved every believer since.

This is why believers are still here.

To be there when the earthquake comes. To be there when the chains fall. To be there when someone falls at their feet and asks the only question that matters.

What must I do to be saved?

The answer has not changed in two thousand years.

Believe in the Lord Jesus Christ, and you will be saved.

Paul was in that prison because he was faithful. He was faithful because he had seen Paradise. He had seen Paradise because he trusted Christ.

And because Paul stayed faithful, a Roman jailer, a pagan, a stranger to the covenants, a man who hours earlier was an enemy, became a brother.

That is the ministry of reconciliation.

That is why we are still here.

Someone, somewhere, is about to ask the question.

Will we be ready to answer?

CONCLUSION

CHAPTER ELEVEN

The Invitation Still Stands

We end where we began.

A hill outside Jerusalem. Three crosses against the sky. Three men dying.

In the middle: Jesus Christ. The Word made flesh. The Lamb of God. At that very moment, defeating Satan, disarming the powers of darkness, destroying death itself.

On one side: a criminal who scoffed. He heard silence. No promise. No Paradise.

On the other side: a criminal who trusted. He heard: "Today you will be with me in Paradise."

Two men. Same opportunity. Different responses. Different eternities.

What We've Seen

Throughout this book, we've traced what Scripture actually teaches.

The myth, the pearly gates, the "good person" standard, and why it's not just wrong, but deadly.

What Scripture reveals, Sheol and Hades, Paradise and Gehenna, resurrection and new creation.

The domain of darkness, Satan as the god of this world, blinding minds, holding captives, and the danger of being given over to a debased mind.

The victory at the cross, Christ disarming the powers, destroying him who had the power of death, silencing the accuser.

Justification by faith, not by works, but by trusting Christ and receiving His righteousness as a gift, just as Abraham believed and it was credited to him as righteousness.

What happens when believers die, immediately with Christ, awaiting resurrection, destined to reign.

What happens when unbelievers die, Hades, the Great White Throne, the lake of fire.

The timeline, Christ's return, resurrection, millennium, new creation.

Why believers are still here, ambassadors, carrying the ministry of reconciliation.

The urgency of now, the door open, but not forever.

It all comes down to this moment. This scene. This question.

Which man?

The Gospel Made Clear

Let it be as clear as possible.

Romans 3:23

> "For all have sinned and fall short of the glory
> of God."

All have sinned. Everyone falls short of God's standard.

Romans 6:23

> "For the wages of sin is death, but the free gift
> of God is eternal life in Christ Jesus our Lord."

Sin earns death. But eternal life is a free gift.

Romans 5:8

> "But God commends his own love toward us,
> in that while we were yet sinners, Christ died
> for us."

While we were sinners. Not after we cleaned up. While we were enemies, Christ died.

Ephesians 2:8-9

"For by grace you have been saved through faith, and that not of yourselves; it is the gift of God, not of works, that no one would boast."

By grace. Through faith. Not of works. The gift of God.

Romans 10:9-10

"...that if you will confess with your mouth that Jesus is Lord and believe in your heart that God raised him from the dead, you will be saved. For with the heart one believes resulting in righteousness; and with the mouth confession is made resulting in salvation."

Believe in the heart. Confess with the mouth. Salvation.

That's the gospel. That's the good news. That's what the man who believed received on the cross.

A Prayer

For anyone wanting to trust Christ, there are no magic words. There is no formula. It's not the prayer that saves, it's Christ who saves.

The prayer is simply how faith is expressed.

But if it helps:

Lord Jesus,

I admit that I am a sinner.

I believe You died for my sins on the cross

and rose from the dead.

I ask You to forgive me.

I trust You as my Savior and my Lord.

Remember me. Take me into Your Kingdom.

Amen.

Nothing More Required

Notice what this does not include.

No rituals. No sacraments. No church membership. No days of obligation. No penance. No probation period.

The man on the cross had none of these. His hands were nailed down. He couldn't do anything except believe.

And it was enough.

Ephesians 2:8-9

> "For by grace you have been saved through faith, and that not of yourselves; it is the gift of God, not of works, that no one would boast."

Nothing more. Nothing added. Christ plus nothing.

That's the gospel.

Does this mean church and baptism and fellowship don't matter? No. They matter deeply. But they are the fruit of salvation, not the root. They flow from a transformed heart, they don't create one.

How to Know You're Saved

Many people pray to receive Christ and then immediately wonder: Did it work? How do I know?

This is an important question. Assurance matters. God does not want His children living in doubt.

1 John 5:13

> "These things I have written to you who believe in the name of the Son of God, that you may know that you have eternal life."

That you may know. Not hope. Not guess. Know.

John wrote his entire letter so that believers could have certainty. Assurance is not arrogance. It is the gift God offers to everyone who trusts in Christ.

So how can someone know?

The Promise of God

First, look at what God has promised.

John 6:37

> "All whom the Father gives me will come to me. He who comes to me I will in no way throw out."

In no way. Under no circumstances. Never. Jesus will not reject anyone who comes to Him.

John 10:28-29

> "I give eternal life to them. They will never perish, and no one will snatch them out of my hand. My Father who has given them to me is greater than all. No one is able to snatch them out of my Father's hand."

Two hands. The Son's hand and the Father's hand. No one can snatch a believer out of either.

If someone has truly come to Christ, truly trusted Him, they are held. Not by their own grip, but by His.

The Witness of the Spirit

Second, there is the internal testimony of the Holy Spirit.

Romans 8:16

> "The Spirit himself testifies with our spirit that we are children of God."

When someone is born again, the Holy Spirit takes up residence in them. And one of His ministries is to assure them that they belong to God.

This is not always a feeling. Feelings come and go. But there is a deep, settled sense that something is different. That they belong to God now. That they are not who they used to be.

2 Corinthians 5:17

> "Therefore if anyone is in Christ, he is a new creation. The old things have passed away. Behold, all things have become new."

A new creation. New desires. New direction. New convictions. The change may be gradual, but it is real.

What About Doubt?

What if someone still doubts? What if they don't feel saved?

Feelings are not the measure. God's Word is the measure.

If someone has genuinely trusted Christ, confessed Him as Lord, believed that God raised Him from the dead, they are saved, whether they feel it or not.

When doubt comes, the answer is not to examine feelings. The answer is to return to Scripture.

John 3:36

"He who believes in the Son has eternal life."

Has. Present tense. Not "will have when he feels it." Has.

The man on the cross may not have felt saved while hanging in agony. He was still dying a criminal's death. His body was broken. His hands were bleeding.

But Jesus said Paradise. And that settled it.

Feelings follow faith. Sometimes quickly, sometimes slowly. But the truth of salvation does not depend on the feeling of salvation.

Believe the Word. The feelings will follow.

What About Peter and the Keys?

Some may ask, "But what about Peter and the keys? Didn't Jesus give Peter authority to bind and loose?"

He did. But look at what Scripture actually says.

The "rock" on which Christ builds His church is not Peter himself, but Peter's confession: "You are the Christ, the Son of the living God" (Matthew 16:16). Peter himself later called Christ the cornerstone, not himself (1 Peter 2:4-6). Paul agreed: "No one can lay any other foundation than that which has been laid, which is Jesus Christ" (1 Corinthians 3:11).

And the authority to bind and loose was given to all the apostles, not Peter alone (Matthew 18:18). Peter used his keys to open the door of the gospel, to Jews, to Samaritans, to Gentiles. He announced the good news. He didn't become a gatekeeper controlling access to heaven.

If any human institution held the keys to salvation, the man on the cross could not have been saved. He never met Peter. He never entered a church. He never received a sacrament.

But Jesus said, "Today you will be with me in Paradise."

No intermediary. No institution. Just Christ and faith.

The End of the Priesthood

Under the Old Covenant, there was a priesthood. Only the high priest could enter the Most Holy Place, and only once a year, with blood for the sins of the people.

A veil, thick and heavy, separated the people from God's presence. It said: You cannot come in. Not yet. Not directly.

But when Christ died, something happened:

Matthew 27:50-51

> "Jesus cried again with a loud voice, and yielded up his spirit. Behold, the veil of the temple was torn in two from the top to the bottom."

From top to bottom. God tore it open. The barrier was removed. Access was granted.

Hebrews 7:24-25

> "But he, because he lives forever, has his priesthood unchangeable. Therefore he is also able to save to the uttermost those who draw near to God through him, seeing that he ever lives to make intercession for them."

One priest. Living forever. Making intercession.

> "For there is one God and one mediator
> between God and men, the man Christ Jesus,
> who gave himself as a ransom for all."

One mediator. Not many. One.

No one needs a human priest to approach God. The veil is torn. Christ is the mediator. He lives forever to intercede.

And every believer is now a priest:

1 Peter 2:9

> "But you are a chosen race, a royal priesthood,
> a holy nation, a people for God's own
> possession, that you may proclaim the
> excellence of him who called you out of
> darkness into his marvelous light."

Every believer. A royal priesthood. Direct access to God.

The Holy Spirit Now In Us

At the moment of belief, something miraculous happens.

Romans 6:6

> "Knowing this, that our old man was crucified
> with him, that the body of sin might be done

away with, so that we would no longer be in bondage to sin."

The old man died with Christ.

Romans 6:4

"We were buried therefore with him through baptism into death, that just as Christ was raised from the dead through the glory of the Father, so we also might walk in newness of life."

The new man rose with Christ.

2 Corinthians 5:17

"Therefore if anyone is in Christ, he is a new creation. The old things have passed away. Behold, all things have become new."

A new creation. Not improved. Not reformed. New.

1 Corinthians 6:19

"Don't you know that your body is a temple of the Holy Spirit who is in you, whom you have from God?"

The Holy Spirit lives in every believer. Not just with them. In them.

Under the Old Covenant, God dwelt in a building. Now He dwells in His people.

Every believer is a temple. Every believer has direct access. Every believer has the Spirit as the guarantee of what is to come.

Cleansed, Justified, Sanctified

At the moment of belief, the believer is:

1 Corinthians 6:11

> "Such were some of you, but you were washed. But you were sanctified. But you were justified in the name of the Lord Jesus, and in the Spirit of our God."

Washed. Cleansed. The blood of Christ removes every stain.

Sanctified. Set apart. Declared holy.

Justified. Declared righteous. Just as Abraham believed and it was credited to him as righteousness.

Hebrews 10:14

> "For by one offering he has perfected forever those who are being sanctified."

Perfected forever. Not working toward perfection. Perfected by Christ's one offering.

Ongoing Cleansing

But what about sin after salvation? What happens when a believer stumbles?

This is the question people are afraid to ask. They believed. They were cleansed. But then they sinned again. Did they lose it? Do they have to start over?

Scripture answers clearly: the cleansing is ongoing.

1 John 1:7

"But if we walk in the light as he is in the light, we have fellowship with one another, and the blood of Jesus Christ his Son cleanses us from all sin."

Notice the tense: cleanses. Present. Ongoing. Continuous.

The believer who walks in the light is being cleansed, moment by moment, by the blood of Christ. Not because they achieve sinless perfection, but because the blood never loses its power.

1 John 1:9

"If we confess our sins, he is faithful and righteous to forgive us our sins and to cleanse us from all unrighteousness."

When believers stumble, and they will, the answer is not despair. The answer is confession. And God, who is faithful, forgives and cleanses.

The man on the cross was cleansed once and entered Paradise that day. He had no time to stumble. But those who live on after salvation are cleansed continually as they walk with Christ. Same blood. Same power. Same Savior.

Direct Access to God

Because of all this, believers can approach God boldly.

Hebrews 10:19-22

> "Having therefore, brothers, boldness to enter into the holy place by the blood of Jesus, by the way which he dedicated for us, a new and living way, through the veil, that is to say, his flesh, and having a great priest over God's house, let's draw near with a true heart in fullness of faith, having our hearts sprinkled from an evil conscience and having our body washed with pure water."

Boldness. Not fear. Not uncertainty. Boldness to enter.

Hebrews 4:16

> "Let's therefore draw near with boldness to the throne of grace, that we may receive mercy and may find grace for help in time of need."

The throne of grace. Direct access. Prayers heard.

Answered Prayer and Full Joy

Christ did not save us to sit idle while we wait for His return. He gave us access to the Father so we could pray, ask in His name, and receive answers.

John 16:24

> "Until now, you have asked nothing in my name. Ask, and you will receive, that your joy may be made full."

That your joy may be made full. Not partial joy. Not just enough to get by. Full joy.

John 15:7

> "If you remain in me, and my words remain in you, you will ask whatever you desire, and it will be done for you."

This is the Christian life: not grim endurance, but joyful partnership with a Father who hears, a Savior who intercedes, and a Spirit who empowers.

The man on the cross had only moments. He received Paradise, but he didn't have time to experience the fullness of walking with Christ, praying in His name, and seeing God move.

We do. That's the privilege of still being here.

Ask. Receive. Let your joy be made full.

Equipped for Spiritual Battle

This access to God is not just for comfort. It is for battle.

We are ambassadors behind enemy lines, and prayer is our weapon.

2 Corinthians 10:4

"For the weapons of our warfare are not of the flesh, but mighty before God to the throwing down of strongholds."

Mighty before God. Throwing down strongholds.

Ephesians 6:18

"With all prayer and requests, praying at all times in the Spirit, and being watchful to this end in all perseverance and requests for all the saints."

Praying at all times in the Spirit. Prayer is woven through all the armor of God.

James 4:7

"Submit yourselves therefore to God. Resist the devil, and he will flee from you."

Resist the devil, and he will flee. This is active, not passive. And it's done through prayer, through the Word, through the authority we have in Christ.

When believers pray in Christ's name, heaven moves. When they resist the devil in faith, he flees. The Spirit who lives in them also intercedes through them, helping their weakness, fighting alongside them.

The man on the cross received Paradise, but he had no time for the battle. We do. We have been equipped, not just saved. Equipped to pray. Equipped to fight. Equipped to stand.

And when we do, our joy is made full, because we see God move, we see strongholds fall, and we see the victory of Christ enforced in our lives and in the lives of those we love.

For Those Who Already Believe

For those who already know Christ, the question remains: Why are you still here?

The mission is clear. The rich man couldn't go back. But believers can go forward.

Who needs to hear? Family? Friends? Neighbors?

They're on the same road the man who scoffed was on. They don't know it.

But believers know. And believers can speak.

Speak while there's still time.

The Middle Cross

Everything comes back to the middle cross.

Jesus Christ, dying for sinners. Defeating Satan. Paying for sin. Conquering death. Opening the door to Paradise.

The man who believed had only one answer when asked by what right he could enter:

"He said I could come."

That's the gospel.

Trust the One on the middle cross. And hear the words every soul longs to hear:

"Today you will be with me in Paradise."

* * *

He had nothing to offer. No works. No credentials. No time.

But he had the word of Christ. And that was everything.

One day, every one of us who has trusted Him will stand in that same place.

And when asked by what right we enter, we will give the same answer.

We will point to the One on the Throne.

The One with the scars in His hands.

The One who hung on the middle cross.

And we will say:

"He said I could come."

APPENDICES

APPENDIX A

Key Scriptures by Topic

The Human Condition

Romans 3:10-12, No one righteous, no one who does good

Romans 3:23, All have sinned and fall short

Ephesians 2:1-3, Dead in sins, following the prince of the air

2 Corinthians 4:4, God of this world has blinded minds

Romans 1:28, Given over to a debased mind

Salvation by Faith

Genesis 15:6, Abraham believed, credited as righteousness

Romans 3:21-24, Justified freely by grace through faith

Romans 4:5, Faith counted as righteousness

Ephesians 2:8-9, By grace through faith, not of works

Romans 10:9-10, Confess and believe, you will be saved

John 5:24, Has passed from death to life

What Christ Accomplished

Colossians 2:13-15, Disarmed principalities, triumphed over them

Hebrews 2:14-15, Destroyed him who had power of death

1 John 3:8, Destroy the works of the devil

2 Corinthians 5:21, The great exchange

Jude 1:9, Michael contending with Satan over Moses

The Believer's Position

2 Corinthians 5:17, New creation in Christ

1 Corinthians 6:11, Washed, sanctified, justified

1 Corinthians 6:19, Body is temple of Holy Spirit

1 Peter 2:9, Royal priesthood

Romans 8:16, Spirit testifies we are children of God

1 John 1:7, Blood of Christ cleanses continually

1 John 1:9, Confess sins, He forgives and cleanses

The Believer's Destiny

2 Corinthians 5:8, Absent from body, at home with Lord

Philippians 1:23, To depart and be with Christ is far better

1 Thessalonians 4:16-17, Dead in Christ rise, caught up together

Revelation 21:1-4, New heaven and earth, God dwells with us

The Unbeliever's Destiny

Luke 16:22-26, Rich man in Hades, great chasm fixed

Revelation 20:11-15, Great White Throne, lake of fire

Matthew 25:46, Eternal punishment, eternal life

The Believer's Mission

2 Corinthians 5:20, Ambassadors for Christ

Matthew 28:19-20, Go make disciples of all nations

Acts 1:8, Witnesses to the ends of the earth

2 Corinthians 6:2, Now is the day of salvation

Prayer and Spiritual Battle

John 16:24, Ask and receive, joy made full

Hebrews 4:16, Boldly approach throne of grace

Ephesians 6:18, Praying at all times in the Spirit

2 Corinthians 10:4, Weapons mighty for throwing down strongholds

James 4:7, Resist the devil, he will flee

Summary Chart

THE BELIEVER'S JOURNEY:

1. Death: Soul immediately with Christ (Paradise)

2. Intermediate State: Conscious joy, awaiting resurrection

3. Christ's Return: Body raised, transformed

4. Judgment Seat of Christ: Rewards given

5. Millennium: Reign with Christ

6. Eternity: New heaven and earth, forever with God

THE UNBELIEVER'S JOURNEY:

1. Death: Soul immediately to Hades (torment)

2. Intermediate State: Conscious suffering, awaiting judgment

3. Great White Throne: Resurrection for judgment

4. Final Judgment: Not found in book of life

5. Lake of Fire: Second death, eternal separation

THE THREE CROSSES:

Christ in the middle: The Savior, the dividing line

Thief who trusted: Paradise that day, eternal life

Thief who scoffed: Silence, Hades, eternal judgment

APPENDIX C
A Simple Gospel Presentation

For sharing the gospel with others:

1. THE PROBLEM: Everyone is a sinner.

"All have sinned and fall short of the glory of God." (Romans 3:23)

No one is good enough. Everyone has failed God's perfect standard.

2. THE PENALTY: Sin leads to death.

"The wages of sin is death." (Romans 6:23a)

Not just physical death, eternal separation from God.

3. THE PROVISION: Christ died for sinners.

"While we were yet sinners, Christ died for us." (Romans 5:8)

He took our punishment. He paid our debt. He died for our sins on the cross.

4. THE PROMISE: Salvation is a free gift.

"The free gift of God is eternal life in Christ Jesus." (Romans 6:23b)

It can't be earned. It can only be received.

5. THE RESPONSE: Believe and confess.

"If you confess with your mouth that Jesus is Lord and believe in your heart that God raised him from the dead, you will be saved." (Romans 10:9)

The man on the cross had nothing but faith. And Jesus said: "Today you will be with me in Paradise."

Discussion Questions

CHAPTER 1: THE MYTH

1. What beliefs about the afterlife are most common in our culture?

2. Why do people find the "good person" myth appealing?

3. What's the danger of believing salvation is about being "good enough"?

CHAPTER 2: WHAT SCRIPTURE REVEALS

1. What surprised you about the Old Testament view of death?

2. How does Hades differ from Gehenna?

3. Why is bodily resurrection so important to the Christian hope?

CHAPTERS 3-4: THE DOMAIN OF DARKNESS / VICTORY AT THE CROSS

1. How does knowing about spiritual warfare change how we see unbelievers?

2. What did Christ accomplish at the cross beyond forgiveness of sins?

3. If Satan is defeated, why is he still active?

CHAPTER 5: JUSTIFICATION BY FAITH

1. Why can't works save?

2. What is "the great exchange"?

3. How does Abraham's faith connect to ours?

CHAPTERS 6-7: THE TWO DESTINIES

1. What happens to believers immediately after death?

2. What does the story of the rich man teach about the urgency of the gospel?

3. How should the reality of hell affect our approach to sharing the gospel?

CHAPTERS 9-10: WHY YOU'RE STILL HERE

1. What does it mean to be an "ambassador for Christ"?

2. Who needs to hear the gospel?

3. What holds people back from sharing it?

CHAPTER 11: WHICH THIEF ARE YOU?

1. Why is nothing more required beyond faith in Christ?

2. What does it mean that every believer is now a priest?

3. How does answered prayer equip us for spiritual battle?

4. How does this book change how you will live?

Frequently Asked Questions

What about people who never heard the gospel?

God is just, and He will judge fairly. Scripture tells us that creation itself reveals God's existence (Romans 1:20), and that God rewards those who earnestly seek Him (Hebrews 11:6). Abraham was declared righteous by faith before the Law, before the cross, before the full revelation of Christ. God knows every heart. But this question should drive urgency, not complacency. The task given to believers is clear: go and tell. The more people hear, the more can respond.

What about babies and children who die?

Scripture gives us hope. When David's infant son died, he said, "I shall go to him, but he will not return to me" (2 Samuel 12:23). David expected to see his child again. Jesus welcomed children and said, "To such belongs the kingdom of God" (Mark 10:14). Children who die before the age of accountability are safe in the arms of Christ. The man on the cross shows that salvation requires personal faith, but those incapable of such faith are covered by God's mercy.

What about deathbed conversions? Is that fair?

The man on the cross is the answer. He lived a life of crime and believed in his final hours. He received Paradise, the same as any lifelong believer. Is that fair? It's grace. The workers hired at the eleventh hour received the same wage as those who worked all day (Matthew 20:1-16). That's not unfair, it's generous. Those who complain about deathbed conversions misunderstand the gospel. Salvation was never a reward for service. It's a gift, and gifts aren't earned.

Can you lose your salvation?

Jesus said, "I give eternal life to them. They will never perish, and no one will snatch them out of my hand" (John 10:28). Paul wrote, "I am persuaded that neither death, nor life, nor angels, nor principalities... nor any other created thing will be able to separate us from the love of God which is in Christ Jesus our Lord" (Romans 8:38-39). Believers are sealed with the Holy Spirit as a guarantee (Ephesians 1:13-14). If salvation could be lost, it would depend on human performance, not Christ's finished work. What Christ finishes, stays finished.

What if I don't feel saved?

Feelings change. Truth doesn't. Salvation is not based on feelings but on the promises of God. "He who believes in the Son has eternal life" (John 3:36). Has, not "feels like he has." If you have trusted Christ, you have eternal life, whether you feel it or not. When doubts come, go back to Scripture, not to your emotions. The man on the cross may not have "felt" saved while hanging in agony. But Jesus said Paradise, and that settled it.

What about baptism? Is it required for salvation?

The man on the cross was never baptized. His hands were nailed down. He couldn't do anything. Yet Jesus said, "Today you will be with me in Paradise." Baptism is important, it's an act of obedience, a public declaration, a picture of death and resurrection with Christ. But it is not what saves. Faith saves. Baptism follows faith as its first act of obedience. The order matters: believe, then be baptized. Not the reverse.

What about good people of other religions?

Jesus said, "I am the way, the truth, and the life. No one comes to the Father except through me" (John 14:6). Peter declared, "There is salvation in no one else, for there is no other name under heaven given among men by which we must be saved" (Acts 4:12). Sincerity doesn't save. Good works don't save. Only Christ saves. This is not arrogance, it's the claim Jesus Himself made. The question is whether He was telling the truth. The empty tomb says He was.

Is there a second chance after death?

"It is appointed for men to die once, and after this, judgment" (Hebrews 9:27). The rich man in Hades begged for relief and was told, "Between us and you there is a great gulf fixed" (Luke 16:26). No crossing over. No second chance. The door is open now. After death, it closes. This is why the urgency of the gospel is real. Today is the day of salvation. Tomorrow is not guaranteed.

What about purgatory?

The word "purgatory" never appears in Scripture. The concept of a middle place where sins are purged after death contradicts the finished work of Christ. "By one offering he has perfected forever those who are being sanctified" (Hebrews 10:14). Perfected forever, not "mostly perfected with some purging left." He went straight to Paradise, not to purgatory. His sins were paid for on the cross beside him. So are ours.

Will we recognize loved ones in heaven?

Yes. When the rich man was in Hades, he recognized Lazarus and Abraham (Luke 16:23). At the Transfiguration, Moses and Elijah appeared and were recognized (Matthew 17:3). Paul expected to be reunited with the Thessalonians (1 Thessalonians 2:19-20). Heaven is not less than earth but more. Relationships will not be erased but fulfilled. We will know and be known.

What if I've sinned too much?

Paul called himself "the chief of sinners" (1 Timothy 1:15). He had persecuted the church, imprisoned believers, and approved of murder. Yet he was saved. The man on the cross was a criminal. Yet he was saved. "Where sin abounded, grace abounded more exceedingly" (Romans 5:20). There is no sin too great for the blood of Christ. If you can still draw breath and believe, you can still be saved.

What about suicide?

Suicide is a tragedy, not an unforgivable sin. The unforgivable sin is persistent rejection of Christ, not a final act of despair. Believers who take their own lives do not lose their salvation. They lose the years of life and service they could have had. If you are struggling with these thoughts, please reach out, to a pastor, a counselor, a friend, or a crisis line. God has more for you. The enemy lies. Don't believe him.

Can the dead communicate with the living?

Scripture forbids attempting to contact the dead (Deuteronomy 18:10-12). The rich man in Hades could not send a message to his brothers, a chasm separated them

(Luke 16:26-31). Any "communication" with the dead is either deception or demonic. The dead in Christ are with Christ. The dead without Christ are in Hades. Neither group is available for conversation. Trust the Word of God, not supposed messages from beyond.

What about near-death experiences?

Some near-death experiences describe light, peace, and even encounters with Christ. Others describe darkness and terror. These experiences are subjective and should never be placed above Scripture. Paul was caught up to Paradise and "heard unspeakable words" (2 Corinthians 12:4), but he didn't build his theology on the experience, he built it on revelation. If a near-death experience contradicts Scripture, reject it. If it confirms Scripture, thank God, but still trust the Word above the experience.

What about cremation vs. burial?

The Bible does not command one over the other. Many godly people in Scripture were buried. Some were burned (1 Samuel 31:12). God will have no trouble resurrecting a cremated body, He who created the body from dust can raise it from ashes. This is a matter of personal or cultural preference, not salvation. Whether buried or cremated, the believer will be raised when Christ returns.

What happens when a believer sins after being saved?

The blood of Christ keeps cleansing. "If we walk in the light as he is in the light, we have fellowship with one another, and the blood of Jesus Christ his Son cleanses us from all sin" (1 John 1:7). The tense is present, ongoing. When believers stumble, they confess: "If we confess our sins, he is faithful and righteous to forgive us our sins and to cleanse us from all unrighteousness" (1 John 1:9). Salvation is not lost. Fellowship is restored through confession. He was cleansed once and went to Paradise. Those who live on are cleansed continually. Same blood. Same power. Same Savior.

The Two Paths: A Visual Timeline

What Happens After Death

THE BELIEVER'S PATH

1. DEATH — The body dies, the soul departs

> "Absent from the body... at home with the Lord" (2 Corinthians 5:8)

2. IMMEDIATELY WITH CHRIST — Paradise

> "Today you will be with me in Paradise" (Luke 23:43)

3. INTERMEDIATE STATE — Conscious joy, rest, fellowship

> "To depart and be with Christ, which is far better" (Philippians 1:23)

4. RESURRECTION — Body raised and transformed

> "The dead in Christ will rise first" (1 Thessalonians 4:16)

5. JUDGMENT SEAT OF CHRIST — Rewards given

"Each one may receive... according to what he has done" (2 Corinthians 5:10)

6. REIGN WITH CHRIST — Millennium

"They will be priests of God and of Christ, and will reign with him" (Revelation 20:6)

7. ETERNITY — New heaven and new earth, God dwelling with His people forever

"Behold, God's dwelling is with people" (Revelation 21:3)

THE UNBELIEVER'S PATH

1. DEATH — The body dies, the soul departs

"It is appointed for men to die once" (Hebrews 9:27)

2. IMMEDIATELY TO HADES — Torment begins

"In Hades, he lifted up his eyes, being in torment" (Luke 16:23)

3. INTERMEDIATE STATE — Conscious suffering, memory, regret

"Between us and you there is a great gulf fixed" (Luke 16:26)

4. RESURRECTION — Body raised for judgment

"Death and Hades gave up the dead who were in them" (Revelation 20:13)

5. GREAT WHITE THRONE — Final judgment

"The dead were judged... according to their works" (Revelation 20:12)

6. LAKE OF FIRE — Second death, eternal separation

"If anyone was not found written in the book of life, he was cast into the lake of fire" (Revelation 20:15)

* * *

THE DIVIDING LINE

Faith in Christ

The man who trusted → Paradise

The man who scoffed → Silence

Scripture Index

All Scripture quotations are from the World English Bible (WEB).

Genesis

Genesis 15:6, Abraham believed, credited as righteousness

Exodus

Exodus 2:12, Moses killed the Egyptian

2 Samuel

2 Samuel 12:23, David: I shall go to him

Psalms

Psalm 6:5, In death there is no memory of you

Psalm 16:10, You will not leave my soul in Sheol

Psalm 49:15, God will redeem my soul from Sheol

Psalm 88:10-12, Do you show wonders to the dead?

Psalm 89:48, Who shall deliver his soul from Sheol?

Ecclesiastes

Ecclesiastes 9:10, No work or knowledge in Sheol

Isaiah

Isaiah 14:9-10, Sheol stirs to meet you

Isaiah 25:8, He has swallowed up death forever

Isaiah 26:19, Your dead shall live

Isaiah 55:6, Seek Yahweh while he may be found

Ezekiel

Ezekiel 33:11, God takes no pleasure in the death of the wicked

Daniel

Daniel 12:2, Some to everlasting life, some to contempt

Matthew

Matthew 7:11, Father gives good gifts to those who ask

Matthew 10:28, Fear him who can destroy both soul and body

Matthew 16:16, You are the Christ, the Son of the living God

Matthew 16:18-19, The keys of the kingdom

Matthew 17:3, Moses and Elijah appeared

Matthew 18:18, Whatever you bind on earth

Matthew 20:1-16, Workers hired at the eleventh hour

Matthew 25:41, Depart into eternal fire

Matthew 25:46, Eternal punishment, eternal life

Matthew 26:42, Jesus prayed in Gethsemane

Matthew 27:50-51, The veil was torn in two

Matthew 28:19-20, Go and make disciples

Mark

Mark 9:47-48, Cast into Gehenna, where the worm doesn't die

Mark 10:14, To such belongs the kingdom of God

Luke

Luke 4:6, Satan: This authority has been delivered to me

Luke 6:12, Jesus prayed all night

Luke 16:19-31, The rich man and Lazarus

Luke 23:39-43, The two men, today you will be with me in Paradise

John

John 3:36, He who believes has eternal life

John 5:24, Has passed out of death into life

John 6:37, I will in no way throw out

John 8:32, The truth will make you free

John 8:44, The devil is a liar and murderer

John 10:28-29, No one will snatch them out of my hand

John 11:25-26, I am the resurrection and the life

John 12:31, The prince of this world will be cast out

John 14:6, I am the way, the truth, and the life

John 14:12-14, Whatever you ask in my name

John 15:7, Ask whatever you desire

John **16:11**, The prince of this world has been judged

John **16:24**, Ask and receive, that your joy may be full

John **19:30**, It is finished

Acts

Acts **1:8**, Witnesses to the ends of the earth

Acts **1:11**, This Jesus will come back

Acts **4:12**, No other name by which we must be saved

Acts **7:55-56**, Stephen saw heaven open

Acts **9:1**, Saul breathing threats

Acts **15:7-11**, Saved through grace

Acts **15:19**, Don't trouble the Gentiles

Acts **17:10-11**, The Bereans examined the Scriptures

Acts **26:18**, Turn from darkness to light

Romans

Romans **1:20**, Creation reveals God

Romans **1:21-28**, God gave them up

Romans **3:10-12**, No one righteous, not one

Romans **3:20**, No flesh justified by works of the law

Romans **3:21-24**, Justified freely by his grace

Romans **3:23**, All have sinned

Romans **4:3-5**, Faith counted as righteousness

Romans **4:23-25**, Written for us who believe

Romans 5:1, Justified by faith, peace with God

Romans 5:8, While we were sinners, Christ died

Romans 5:20, Where sin abounded, grace abounded more

Romans 6:1-2, Shall we continue in sin?

Romans 6:4, Walk in newness of life

Romans 6:6, Our old man was crucified

Romans 6:23, Wages of sin is death, gift of God is eternal life

Romans 8:1, No condemnation in Christ Jesus

Romans 8:9, The Spirit dwells in you

Romans 8:16, The Spirit testifies we are children of God

Romans 8:26, The Spirit intercedes

Romans 8:33-34, Who could bring a charge?

Romans 8:37-39, More than conquerors

Romans 10:9-10, Confess and believe

Romans 10:17, Faith comes by hearing

Romans 11:13, Apostle to Gentiles

1 Corinthians

1 Corinthians 2:7-8, Rulers did not understand

1 Corinthians 3:11, No other foundation than Christ

1 Corinthians 6:11, Washed, sanctified, justified

1 Corinthians 6:19, Body is temple of the Holy Spirit

1 Corinthians 15:8, Christ appeared to Paul last

1 Corinthians 15:51-57, We will all be changed

2 Corinthians

2 Corinthians 4:3-4, The god of this world has blinded minds

2 Corinthians 5:8, Absent from body, at home with Lord

2 Corinthians 5:10, Judgment seat of Christ

2 Corinthians 5:17, New creation in Christ

2 Corinthians 5:18-20, Ministry of reconciliation

2 Corinthians 5:21, Made to be sin, become righteousness

2 Corinthians 6:2, Now is the day of salvation

2 Corinthians 10:3-5, Weapons mighty before God

2 Corinthians 12:4, Caught up into Paradise

Galatians

Galatians 1:11-12, Received by revelation

Galatians 1:15-17, Arabia, alone with Christ

Galatians 2:11, Paul rebuked Peter

Galatians 2:16, Not justified by works of the law

Galatians 2:20, Crucified with Christ

Galatians 2:21, If righteousness through law, Christ died for nothing

Ephesians

Ephesians 1:13-14, Sealed with the Holy Spirit

Ephesians 2:1-3, Dead in sins, children of wrath

Ephesians 2:5-6, Made alive together with Christ

Ephesians 2:8-9, By grace through faith

Ephesians 2:10, Created for good works

Ephesians 2:20, Christ the cornerstone

Ephesians 3:8, Preach to Gentiles

Ephesians 3:20, Exceedingly abundantly above all we ask

Ephesians 6:11, Put on the whole armor of God

Ephesians 6:12, Wrestling against principalities

Ephesians 6:18, Praying at all times

Philippians

Philippians 1:21-23, To depart and be with Christ

Philippians 3:20, Our citizenship is in heaven

Colossians

Colossians 1:13-14, Delivered from darkness, translated into Kingdom

Colossians 2:13-15, Disarmed principalities, triumphed over them

Colossians 3:1, Raised together with Christ

1 Thessalonians

1 Thessalonians 2:19-20, Reunited with believers

1 Thessalonians 4:13, Do not grieve as those without hope

1 Thessalonians 4:16-17, Dead in Christ rise first

1 Timothy

1 Timothy 1:15, Chief of sinners

1 Timothy 2:5-6, One mediator between God and men

2 Timothy

2 Timothy 2:25-26, Taken captive by the devil

Hebrews

Hebrews 2:14-15, Destroy him who had power of death

Hebrews 3:15, Today if you hear his voice

Hebrews 4:16, Draw near to the throne of grace

Hebrews 7:24-25, Unchangeable priesthood

Hebrews 8:1, High priest sat down

Hebrews 9:14, Cleanse conscience from dead works

Hebrews 9:27, Appointed to die once, then judgment

Hebrews 10:10, Sanctified through offering

Hebrews 10:14, Perfected forever

Hebrews 10:19-22, Boldness to enter the holy place

Hebrews 11:6, God rewards those who seek him

James

James 4:7, Resist the devil, he will flee

James 4:14, Life is a vapor

1 Peter

1 Peter 2:4-6, Christ the cornerstone

1 Peter 2:5, Holy priesthood

1 Peter 2:9, Royal priesthood

1 Peter 2:11, Foreigners and pilgrims

2 Peter

2 Peter 3:9, Not wanting anyone to perish

1 John

1 John 1:7, Blood cleanses from all sin

1 John 1:9, Confess sins, He forgives

1 John 3:8, Destroy the works of the devil

1 John 4:1, Test the spirits

1 John 5:13, That you may know you have eternal life

Jude

Jude 1:9, Michael contending with the devil over Moses

Revelation

Revelation 1:6, Kingdom of priests

Revelation 12:10, Accuser of the brothers

Revelation 12:12, The devil has great wrath

Revelation 20:6, Reign with Christ a thousand years

Revelation 20:10, Devil thrown into lake of fire

Revelation 20:11-15, Great White Throne judgment

Revelation 21:1-4, New heaven and new earth

Revelation 21:5, Behold, I make all things new

APPENDIX H

Paul's Ministry — Not One of the Twelve

The Apostle Paul occupies a unique position in biblical history. Unlike the Twelve Apostles who walked with Jesus during His earthly ministry, Paul received his gospel by direct revelation from the risen Christ (Galatians 1:11-12). He was called specifically to be the apostle to the Gentiles (Romans 11:13), and much of what we understand about grace, justification by faith, and the mystery of the Church comes through his letters. This timeline illustrates the distinct nature of Paul's ministry alongside Christ's earthly ministry and the ministry of the Twelve.

Biblical Timeline: Ministries of Christ, the Twelve Apostles, and Paul

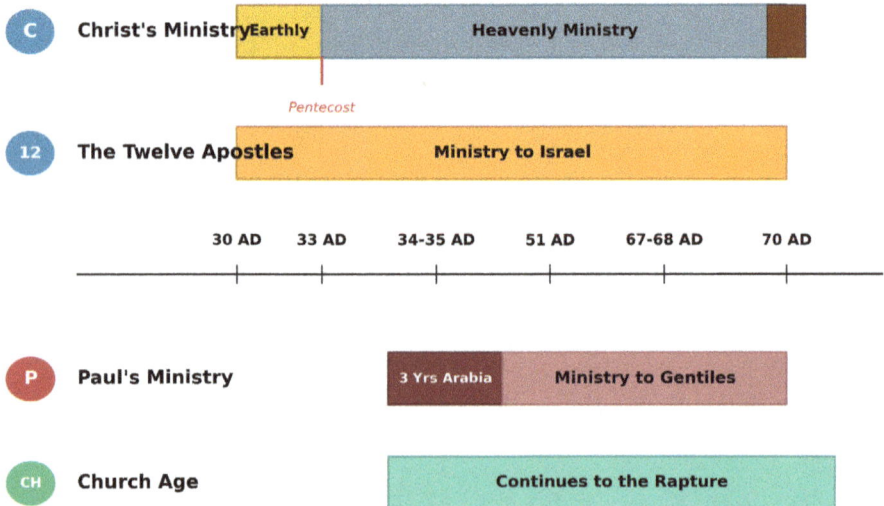

C — Christ's Ministry — Earthly — Heavenly Ministry

Pentecost

12 — The Twelve Apostles — Ministry to Israel

30 AD   33 AD   34-35 AD   51 AD   67-68 AD   70 AD

P — Paul's Ministry — 3 Yrs Arabia — Ministry to Gentiles

CH — Church Age — Continues to the Rapture

239

APPENDIX I

Understanding Biblical Time

Scripture presents history as moving toward a purposeful end. From creation through the present Church Age to the future Kingdom, God's plan unfolds according to His sovereign timetable. Daniel was given specific revelation about "seventy weeks" determined for Israel (Daniel 9:24-27), with the Church Age representing a prophetic pause — the "mystery" hidden in ages past but now revealed (Ephesians 3:1-6). The same Christ who saved the criminal on the cross continues to offer salvation today, during this age of grace.

Biblical Timeline According to Dispensationalism

With Focus on Prophetic Interruption and Future Fulfillment

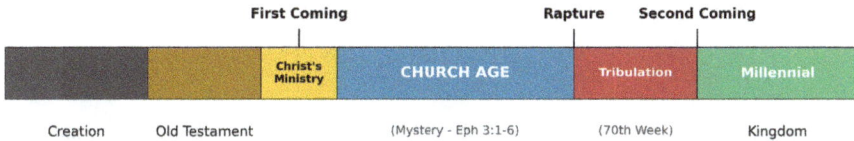

First Coming		Rapture	Second Coming

		Christ's Ministry	CHURCH AGE	Tribulation	Millennial

| Creation | Old Testament | | (Mystery - Eph 3:1-6) | (70th Week) | Kingdom |

Daniel's 70 Weeks (Daniel 9:24-27)

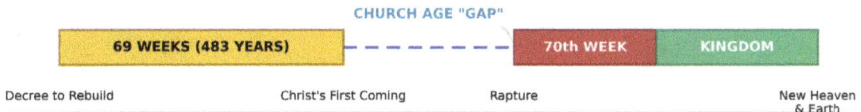

CHURCH AGE "GAP"

69 WEEKS (483 YEARS)	- - - - - - -	70th WEEK	KINGDOM

| Decree to Rebuild | Christ's First Coming | Rapture | New Heaven & Earth |

The "This Generation" Issue (Matthew 24:34)

- Jesus said: "This generation shall not pass, till all these things be fulfilled"
- The fulfillment was conditional on Israel's acceptance of Christ
- When Israel rejected Christ, prophecy was suspended, not cancelled

www.ingramcontent.com/pod-product-compliance
Lightning Source LLC
Chambersburg PA
CBHW062057080426
42734CB00012B/2678